The economic impacts of tax—transfer policy

Regional and distributional effects

Institute for Research on Poverty
Monograph Series

The economic impacts of tax—transfer policy

Regional and distributional effects

Fredrick L. Golladay
Robert H. Haveman

Institute for Research on Poverty
Madison, Wisconsin

with the assistance of Kevin Hollenbeck

ACADEMIC PRESS   New York   San Francisco   London

A Subsidiary of Harcourt Brace Jovanovich, Publishers

This book is one of a series sponsored by the Institute for Research on Poverty of the University of Wisconsin pursuant to the provisions of the Economic Opportunity Act of 1964.

ACADEMIC PRESS, INC.
111 Fifth Avenue, New York, New York 10003

United Kingdom Edition published by
ACADEMIC PRESS, INC. (LONDON) LTD.
24/28 Oval Road, London NW1

Library of Congress Cataloging in Publication Data

Golladay, Fredrick L.
      The economic impacts of tax-transfer policy.

      (Institute for Research on Poverty monograph series)
      Includes bibliographical references.
      1.   Negative income tax–United States–Mathematical models.   2.   Income distribution–United States–Mathematical models.   I.   Haveman, Robert H., joint author.   II.   Title.   III.   Series: Wisconsin. University–Madison. Institute for Research on Poverty. Monograph series.
HC110.P63G64   1976   339.2   76-13938
ISBN 0–12–288850–2

PRINTED IN THE UNITED STATES OF AMERICA

The Institute for Research on Poverty is a national center for research established at the University of Wisconsin in 1966 by a grant from the Office of Economic Opportunity. Its primary objective is to foster basic, multidisciplinary research into the nature and causes of poverty and means to combat it.

In addition to increasing the basic knowledge from which policies aimed at the elimination of poverty can be shaped, the Institute strives to carry analysis beyond the formulation and testing of fundamental generalizations to the development and assessment of relevant policy alternatives.

The Institute endeavors to bring together scholars of the highest caliber whose primary research efforts are focused on the problem of poverty, the distribution of income, and the analysis and evaluation of social policy, offering staff members wide opportunity for interchange of ideas, maximum freedom for research into basic questions about poverty and social policy, and dissemination of their findings.

Contents

List of tables

xi

Foreword

While income-maintenance programs are designed to reduce poverty and economic insecurity, they have other effects as well. They may alter savings, consumption behavior, and even living arrangements. Moreover, such programs may indirectly alter what goods and services are demanded by consumers, where these goods and services are produced, and who is employed to produce them. In this book, Fredrick Golladay and Robert Haveman are concerned with the latter kinds of effects. They present an empirical simulation model designed to estimate the microeconomic effects of income-transfer programs on regions, industries, occupations, and the distribution of income, and employ the model in evaluating proposed income-transfer policies.

The direct effects of income-maintenance programs clearly favor the poor. But the degree to which various income classes ultimately benefit from programs is not obvious. Nor is it evident how changes in consumption and production patterns induced by transfers affect various regions, industries, or occupations. Do the increased goods and services purchased by program beneficiaries come from industries that employ large concentrations of low-skill labor? Does redistributing income from high-income regions toward less developed regions create more jobs for people living in relatively low-income regions? Or do the indirect effects favor developed regions and high-income workers? Considering only the direct effects may lead to a misestimation of how much income-maintenance programs help the poor.

The model developed in this study contains substantially more sectoral detail than is usual in estimating the distributional effects of policy changes. It explicitly estimates policy-induced patterns of consumer demand, the structure of interindustry relationships, and the occupational and skill requirements of altered industry outputs. As a result, the model makes it possible to compare a policy's indirect distributional consequences with its direct consequences and, more importantly, to compare the income distribution created by the sum of the direct and indirect effects with the income distribution that existed prior to the policy change.

In the book, the direct and indirect effects of two variants of a negative income tax plan are analyzed: a "standard" negative income

xiii

tax (NIT) and the Nixon Administration's proposed Family Assistance Plan (FAP). The distributions of the benefits of the hypothetical programs are estimated by simulating the application of their eligibility rules and benefit schedules to a national sample survey of households. Financing for both plans is assumed to come from a proportional increase in the federal personal income tax. Although the programs analyzed are hypothetical ones, the methodology and results are more generally applicable.

During the four years of work that resulted in this volume, Robert Haveman was the director, and Fredrick Golladay was a staff member, of the Institute for Research on Poverty. Their study should be viewed as part of a larger corpus of Institute research on income-maintenance programs. The effects of such programs on work effort was the central question of the New Jersey and the Rural Income-Maintenance Experiments conducted by the Institute. Other volumes in the Institute's Monograph Series have reported on the effects of income-maintenance programs on work effort and analyzed the problems created by the multiplicity of income-maintenance programs. The present volume, by tracing through the indirect effects of income-maintenance programs on regions, industries, and occupations, contributes to our growing knowledge about the effects and the effectiveness of alternative income-maintenance programs.

Irwin Garfinkel
Director, Institute for
Research on Poverty

Preface

In discourse about public programs, the issue of equity has begun to compete with the more traditional issue of allocative efficiency. While this shifting emphasis is most evident in debates about income redistribution policy, it has also affected the application of public expenditure analysis more generally. Economists, while professing interest in both the efficiency and the equity of public outlays, have tended to focus attention on the resource allocation impacts of public measures; benefit–cost analysis and cost–effectiveness analysis have been widely applied in planning and evaluation. Until recently, the impact of the public sector on the distribution of economic welfare has attracted comparatively little interest. As a result, methods of analyzing it are not yet as fully developed or as broad in scope as those applied in evaluating efficiency effects. While efforts have been made to identify direct beneficiaries of public programs and to introduce into benefit–cost analysis weighting schemes reflecting the relative social importance of income flows to various groups of citizens, both of these are ad hoc approaches to the issue of equity.

The study presented in this volume is intended to provide more general and hence more useful information about the impact of proposed reforms in income-maintenance programs on the size distribution of income. Rather than an attempt to integrate efficiency and equity analyses, it is a detailed tracing of the efficiency (output) and income distributional effects of transfer payments and the taxes that pay for them, through an economy-wide microsimulation model. The model results in no ideal solution to the problem of inequity, but it does provide the kind of information policymakers need about the dynamic, direct and indirect implications of income redistribution.

Acknowledgments

We are deeply indebted to a number of individuals and institutions for guidance in obtaining and interpreting data and for assistance in constructing components of what has come to be a very large model. We wish to acknowledge the help of the Urban Institute, particularly John Moeller (now at the University of Maine) and Jodie Allen (now at Mathematica Policy Research), Karen Polenske of the Massachusetts Institute of Technology, and Roger H. Bezdek of the Bureau of Economic Analysis. David Betson, Marc Freiman, Marilyn Manser, Rafiq Omar and, especially, Nancy Schofield and Nancy Williamson provided research and computer programming assistance. Advice on various aspects of the modeling was provided by John Bishop, Glen Cain, Laurits Christiansen, Arthur Goldberger, Charles Palit, and Eugene Smolensky, all of the University of Wisconsin–Madison. Several times during the course of the study, the participants in the weekly seminar of the Institute for Research on Poverty provided helpful commentary.

Our largest debt is owed to Kevin Hollenbeck of Mathematica Policy Research, who worked for two years as a research assistant on the project while a graduate student at the University of Wisconsin–Madison. Several parts of the study—including the formalization of the model and the empirical estimation of distribution effects—are as much his product as ours.

Helpful reviews and critiques of earlier versions of the manuscript were received from Anne Carter of Brandeis University, Stephen Dresch of Yale University, Karen Polenske of the Massachusetts Institute of Technology, and Jeffrey Williamson of the University of Wisconsin–Madison.

Finally, our thanks to the members of the secretarial and editorial staffs of the Institute for Research on Poverty. Susan Elbe, Catherine Ersland, and Marlene Kundert were primarily responsible for typing the several incarnations of the manuscript. Whatever degree of clarity of style present in the volume is due largely to the careful editing of Camille Smith. Finally, the help of Beverly Neupert in scheduling the numerous meetings of the participants in the project and, in general, keeping administrative details well-ordered is acknowledged.

Income transfers and income redistribution

Programs of income maintenance and income redistribution now
account for about 40 percent of a $350 billion federal budget. This
represents a nearly tenfold increase since 1950, when income-support
payments were but $13 million. In the same 25 years, the number of
beneficiaries has risen from about 16 million to over 60 million. Social
Security is the largest of these programs, with nearly $60 million of bene-
fits paid annually to nearly 30 million beneficiaries. Other important
programs in the system include Supplemental Security Insurance (SSI),
Medicare, Medicaid, Food Stamps, and Aid to Families with Dependent
Children (AFDC).[1]

Taken together, these programs and the taxes required for their
financing are an important determinant of the shape of the distribution
of disposable income among households in the United States. Because
the benefits of most of these programs are aimed at low-income families,
they are important in reducing the incidence of poverty; it has been

---

[1]For a description of these programs and their growth, see Charles L. Schultze et al.,
Setting National Priorities: The 1974 Budget (Washington, D.C.: The Brookings Institution,
1974), Chapter 3.

estimated that over 40 percent of the 15 million poor American families are lifted out of poverty by these programs.[2] For the same reason, the distribution of income after transfers and taxes is substantially less unequal than the distribution of pretransfer income. It is largely because of the rapid growth of these programs in the last decade that the increasing inequality in the distribution of earned (or pretransfer) income has not been reflected in the distribution of final (or posttransfer) income or in an increase in the poverty population.[3]

Within the last decade, the transfer system has been the subject of substantial evaluation and research. Numerous studies have been conducted of the effects of the system on both economic behavior and the distribution of income. These studies have attempted to identify the incentives implicit in the programs and to measure behavioral responses to these incentives. Those studies concerned with the distributive impacts of the programs have measured the incidence of program benefits and costs among groups categorized by income level, race, region, and age. The emphasis of many of these studies has been on "target efficiency"—the extent to which benefits are received by individuals designated as the targets of the programs.

The most extensive efforts to measure behavioral effects have focused on the impacts of the current system or proposed revisions of it on work effort or labor supply.[4] These efforts have culminated in a number of social experiments designed to test the work response of families to income-support payments within rigorous, controlled experiments. By and large, these studies have found that groups with strong attachments to the labor force (prime-aged male family heads, for example) are not very responsive to the incentives implicit in these

[2]See James N. Morgan et al., *Five Thousand American Families—Patterns of Economic Progress*, vol. 1 (Ann Arbor: University of Michigan, Institute for Social Research, Survey Research Center, 1974). These results are summarized in Michael C. Barth et al., *Toward an Effective Income Support System: Problems, Prospects, and Choices* (Madison: University of Wisconsin, Institute for Research on Poverty, 1974).

[3]The role of the income-support system in reducing poverty and equalizing the distribution of income is documented in Timothy M. Smeeding, "Measuring the Economic Welfare of Low Income Households and The Anti-Poverty Effectiveness of Cash and Non-Cash Transfer Programs" (Ph.D. dissertation, University of Wisconsin-Madison, 1975); and Robert D. Plotnick and Felicity Skidmore, *Progress Against Poverty: A Review of the 1964–1974 Decade*, Institute for Research on Poverty Monograph Series (New York: Academic Press, 1975).

[4]For a review of the results of several cross-sectional estimates of labor supply effects, see Glen G. Cain and Harold W. Watts, eds., *Income Maintenance and Labor Supply* (New York: Rand–McNally, 1973).

programs, while groups with weaker labor force attachments (spouses, the aged, and female family heads) are considerably more responsive. The New Jersey Income-Maintenance Experiment, for example, determined that prime-aged male family heads adjusted the quantity of their labor to a minor (and statistically insignificant) extent under income-transfer schemes with various degrees of built-in work disincentive.[5]

While none of the other anticipated behavioral responses has been analyzed within an experimental research design, cross-sectional, observational studies have been undertaken, including analyses of changes in family structure, fertility, and migration in response to the incentives of income transfers. Generally, these studies have indicated that recipient families do respond to the incentives implicit in transfer programs. Higher welfare payments, for example, are associated with larger proportions of mothers raising children without husbands and of already broken families establishing separate households.[6] Studies of the fertility effects of income-transfer policies have identified substantial financial inducements for single women and couples to have additional children, although the strength of the response to this incentive has not been reliably estimated.[7] Similarly, while studies of geographic disparities in program benefits have documented the existence and size of the program-induced incentive to migrate, the extent to which actual

[5]Harold W. Watts et al., "The Labor Supply Response of Husbands," *Journal of Human Resources* 9 (Spring 1974):181–200. See also Joseph Pechman and P. Michael Timpane, eds., *Work Incentives and Income Guarantees: The New Jersey Negative Income Tax Experiment* (Washington, D.C.: The Brookings Institution, 1975).

[6]For a review of this evidence, see Robert I. Lerman, "The Family, Poverty, and Welfare Programs: An Introductory Essay on Problems of Analysis and Policy," in U.S. Congress, Joint Economic Committee, Subcommittee on Fiscal Policy, "The Family, Poverty, and Welfare Programs: Factors Affecting Family Stability," Studies in Public Welfare, Paper no. 12, part 1, Joint Committee Print (Washington, D.C.: U.S. Government Printing Office, 1973), pp. 1–36, (Y4.Ec7:W45/paper 12/pt. 1). See also Marjorie Honig, "AFDC Income, Recipient Rates, and Family Dissolution," *Journal of Human Resources* 9 (Summer 1974):303–322, and Phillips Cutright and John Scanzoni, "Income Supplements and the American Family," in U.S. Congress, Joint Economic Committee, Subcommittee on Fiscal Policy, "Factors Affecting Family Stability," pp. 54–89.

[7]Glen G. Cain has developed a rough estimate of a 15 percent increase in fertility due to the reduction in the costs of children attributable to income-maintenance programs. This response would be expected from those family units covered by income-maintenance programs—about 15 percent of the total population. See Glen G. Cain, "The Effect of Income Maintenance Laws on Fertility in the United States," in U.S. Commission on Population Growth and the American Future, *Aspects of Population Growth Policy*, ed. Robert Parke, Jr., and Charles F. Westoff, Commission Research Reports, vol. 6 (Washington, D.C.: U.S. Government Printing Office, 1972), pp. 325–373, (Y3.P81:9/6).

migration has been motivated by this incentive (as opposed to other spatial factors) is still unsettled.[8]

Studies of the distributional impact of the income-transfer system have sought to isolate the characteristics of the recipients of program benefits.[9] While these analyses have documented the substantial benefits provided to poor families by the system, they also have revealed numerous horizontal and vertical inequities. Some programs have been found to have high antipoverty effectiveness (AFDC, for example); others have distributed the bulk of their benefits to families of middle or upper-middle income (Unemployment Compensation, for example). Some poor groups—low-income, male-headed families with children, in particular—receive few benefits even if they are active in the labor force. These studies have also shown that the measured antipoverty effectiveness of income-support programs depends significantly on the indicator of economic status used to rank families. A program showing a high concentration of benefits to families that are poor as measured by current income may be relatively ineffective in meeting the needs of families with low earnings capacity.[10]

The study presented in this monograph is in the tradition of these earlier studies of behavioral response and distributional impact. However, while previous investigations have measured only the primary response to or incidence of the programs, this study is an attempt to trace the sequence of responses and the incidence of effects of income-transfer policies throughout the economic system. It provides a numerical analysis of the microeconomic effects of redistributing purchasing power through a uniform, national program of income supplementation

[8]John F. Kain and Robert Schaefer have presented some of the most recent estimates of the effects of income-maintenance policy on migration. See their "Income Maintenance, Migration, and Regional Growth," *Public Policy* 20 (Spring 1972): 199–225.

[9]See Robert J. Lampman, "How Much Does the American System of Transfers Benefit the Poor," in *Economic Progress and Social Welfare*, ed. Leonard H. Goodman (New York: Columbia University Press, 1966); Irene Lurie, "Transfer Payments and Income Maintenance," U.S. President's Commission on Income Maintenance Programs, Staff Paper, mimeographed (Washington, D.C., 1969); Benjamin Okner, "Transfer Payments: Their Distribution and Their Role in Reducing Poverty," in *Redistribution to the Rich and the Poor: The Grants Economics of Income Distribution*, ed. Kenneth E. Boulding and Martin Pfaff (Belmont, Calif.: Wadsworth Publishing, 1972); and Schultze et al., *Setting National Priorities*. See also Smeeding, "Measuring Economic Welfare," and Plotnick and Skidmore, *Progress Against Poverty*.

[10]See Irwin Garfinkel and Robert H. Haveman, "Earnings Capacity and the Target Efficiency of Alternative Transfer Programs," *American Economic Review* 64 (May 1974): 196–204.

for the poor. In so doing, it estimates both the effects of a program on output and employment—by region, occupation, and industry—and the shifts in income distribution induced by these indirect effects.

In Chapter 2, the tax–transfer programs to be simulated are described. They include both a simple negative income tax plan (NIT), and the more complex series of policy changes implied by late versions of the Nixon Administration's Family Assistance Plan (H.R. 1).

Chapters 3 and 4 present a description of the several parts of the model, emphasizing both conceptual issues (Chapter 3) and empirical procedures (Chapter 4). In these discussions the assumptions underlying each part of the model are specified and the data bases supporting each part are described. The sequential and short-run structure of the model is emphasized.

Chapters 5 and 6 present the principal findings of the analysis. Chapter 5 compares the indirect distributional effects of the policy with both the income distribution existing prior to the policy change and the income distribution after the policy's primary, or direct, distributional effects. Chapter 6 examines some of the industrial, occupational, and regional effects that intervene between the primary and final distributional impacts.

Finally, Chapter 7 summarizes the results of the study and appraises the structure of the model. Although the model is not a complete general equilibrium model, it does yield a more comprehensive estimate of the total distributional impact of tax–transfer policy than has heretofore been available.

2 _____

Two tax–transfer policy proposals—the basis for a simulation exercise

Recent and proposed changes in federal tax and transfer policies have been devised to achieve income redistribution. In this chapter, two reforms explicitly designed to aid the poor are described. The economic effects of these programs and their impacts on the distribution of income are analyzed in empirical simulations reported in subsequent chapters. Given the explicit antipoverty objectives of these proposals, simulation estimates of their regional, occupational, and distributional effects are of particular interest.

Two tax–transfer proposals

Both proposals analyzed in this study are variants of a negative income tax plan. They differ, however, in the income base employed in determining benefits, in the rate at which program benefits are reduced in response to income receipts from other sources, and in the assumptions made regarding the continuation or elimination of other public transfer programs. The distributions of the benefits of the two programs are estimated by simulating the application of their eligibility rules and benefit schedules to a national sample survey of households.

7

A "standard" negative income tax

The first transfer proposal is a negative income tax plan designed to provide income support to all families with children. For a family of four persons, this plan guarantees an income of $2400; for larger and smaller families, the income guarantee varies from this level by a fixed dollar amount per adult and per child, up to a certain limit.[1] Beyond an earnings level of $720, family benefits are reduced by $.67 for each additional dollar of earned income and by $.60 for each additional dollar of unearned income. At an earnings level of about $4300, benefits for a family of four with no unearned income fall to zero. Figure 2.1 shows this benefit structure for a family of four with only earned income, illustrating the reduction in government benefits as earned income rises.

Integration of this proposal with other transfer programs is achieved by counting benefits received from the other programs as income and reducing negative income tax payments accordingly. Thus the proposal does not require abolition or change of any other programs.

A number of additional eligibility and benefit provisions are incorporated into this program. Some of these are explicit provisions of

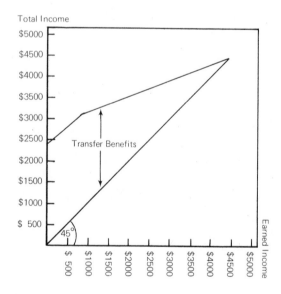

FIGURE 2.1. Negative income tax benefits for a family of four persons with no unearned income.

[1]The benefit formula is described in Appendix A.

welfare legislation that has been proposed by the federal government; others are assumed to be part of the program for purposes of this study.

1. Household units headed by college students are eliminated from eligibility, as are institutionalized persons and those in the military.
2. One hundred percent of those eligible for the program are assumed to participate.
3. The accounting period for determining benefits is one year.

The Family Assistance Plan (FAP)

The second transfer program to be analyzed is the Nixon Administration's Family Assistance Plan, as modified by the House Ways and Means Committee in its 1971 legislative proposal commonly referred to as H.R. 1.[2]

This plan combines three changes in transfer policy. First, it introduces a federal benefit program with a benefit structure conditioned on earnings, as in the negative income tax.[3] Benefits are reduced by $.67 for each dollar of earned income beyond $720 and for each dollar of alimony income. In addition, benefits are reduced dollar-for-dollar for unearned income other than categorical public assistance benefits.[4] Second, existing family-based welfare programs—Aid to Families with Dependent Children (AFDC and AFDC-UP) and Food Stamps—are eliminated. Finally, individual states are permitted to supplement federal benefits up to an amount equal to previous state costs of welfare programs.[5]

Because of data limitations, a number of specific provisions of

[2] In particular, this plan is that part of H.R. 1 described in the "Opportunities for Families" and "Family Assistance Programs" sections of Title XXI of the bill.

[3] As indicated in Appendix A, children's income is treated differently in this plan than in the negative income tax plan described.

[4] The benefit formula is described in Appendix A.

[5] In simulating the state supplementation aspect of the full program, it is assumed that supplementary payments are made to all family units eligible for AFDC and AFDC-UP (whether or not they were recipients) to insure that they are not worse off after the policy changes than before. In general, for covered families of any given size, chargeable income is compared with the state maximum AFDC or AFDC-UP payment and any deficit is assigned as a supplemental benefit. In addition, the observed maximum payment for each state is adjusted upward by an amount equivalent to the Food Stamp bonus evaluated at the former maximum benefit levels. A more detailed description of the procedure adopted for estimating supplemental payments is presented in Appendix B.

H.R. 1 are not incorporated into the analysis.[6] The supplementary eligibility and benefit provisions of the negative income tax proposal are applied to this proposal as well.

Financing the transfer proposals

Financing for both the negative income tax plan and the Family Assistance Plan is assumed to come from a proportional increase in effective tax rates of the federal personal income tax. The assumptions adopted to estimate the distribution of this increased tax burden among families are fairly straightforward. First, on the basis of federal personal-income tax schedules, standard deduction and low-income allowance provisions, and reported gross income and exemptions, total federal taxes paid by each individual household are estimated. Second, a proportional tax increase is assumed, and each family's estimated federal tax liability is raised by the percentage increase in total taxes required to finance the program.[7]

While this procedure approximates the distributional impact of the federal income tax, it neglects several significant aspects of the tax structure that lead to variation in the tax liability of families within any income class. In particular, using the standard deduction rather than itemizing deductions understates actual claims of contributions to charitable organizations, deductable interest expenses, taxes paid to state and local governments, and allowable health expenditures by middle- and upper-income households. The treatment in the simulation of capital gains on the sale of assets ignores the special provisions of the capital gains tax. The effect of these simplifications is to understate the tax liabilities of upper-income households.

The assumption that the transfer scheme will be financed by such a tax increase is arbitrary, but it may be justified by the uncertainty regarding the source of funds for financing any given government

---

[6]Ways in which the analyzed plan differs from H.R. 1 include the following: (1) Irregular receipts of earned and unearned income, child care costs, training allowances, foster child care payments, and tuition and fees are excluded from our definitions of income and exclusions; (2) no resource (asset) test for eligibility is employed; (3) family members available for employment but not working are not excluded from the family unit; and (4) self-employed persons with high gross incomes are not excluded from eligibility.

[7]A more detailed specification of the procedures followed in estimating the distribution of the taxes required to finance the transfer programs is found in Appendix C.

program. Indeed, the financing of a policy change need not require a change in the tax structure at all; increases in the effective tax rate brought about by a progressive rate structure and inflation, reductions in other public expenditure programs, and increases in revenues due to economic growth are all possible sources of funds. Moreover, even if it were known that an increase in a particular tax was to finance the program, it would be difficult to determine the distribution of the costs of the increase from data on the existing distribution of the costs of that tax; thus computational expediency argues for a proportional increase in the existing federal income tax.[8]

On evaluating tax–transfer policies

Antipoverty transfer programs of the sort just described have been viewed by many as attractive instruments for achieving a less unequal income distribution, or a smaller incidence of poverty, in the nation.

The simplest defense of this view focuses only on the distribution of direct benefits and costs and neglects the distributional effects of other economic changes induced by the program. Because the direct effects favor the poor, it is presumed that the postprogram income distribution will be more nearly equal than the preprogram distribution. A somewhat less naive view recognizes that other economic changes will occur but concludes that these changes are sufficiently complex to warrant the assumption that they will cancel each other out and leave the net distributional effect of the policy dominated by direct impacts.

Alternatively, one might judge that the indirect effects will add to the equalizing impact of the direct redistribution. The direct redistribution, it might be observed, will favor poorer, less developed regions and will siphon purchasing power away from higher-income regions. The resulting reallocation of labor demands from the richer to the poorer regions might be expected to yield net benefits for lower-skill, lower-income workers. Similarly, impact in favor of the poor can be expected if the goods and services purchased by program beneficiaries are produced by lower-skill occupations while those who bear the cost of the program reduce their purchase of goods requiring higher-skill inputs. If these conditions are met, the total equalizing effect—direct

---

[8]For a discussion of the difficulty of estimating the distribution of tax costs for financing any public program, see W. Lee Hansen and Burton A. Weisbrod, "Who Pays for a Public Expenditure Program?" *National Tax Journal* 24 (December 1971):515–517.

plus indirect impacts—will be greater than the equalizing effect of the direct distribution of benefits and tax costs alone.

Indeed, the view that direct cash transfers are effective antipoverty instruments might be sustained even if the indirect impacts favored the rich. Such policies might have a substantial equalizing effect even if the increased expenditures of beneficiaries stimulated high-wage sectors and the reduced expenditures of cost bearers depressed the demand for low-wage sectors and low-skill occupations. These indirect effects, while favoring the rich, might be smaller than the direct impacts, leaving the net effect of the policy favoring the poor.

Finally, it is possible that all of these hypotheses that such policies are effective against poverty are in error. The direct effects, while designed to favor the poor, might be swamped by indirect effects favoring high-income families relative to low-income families. In this case, the net distributional impact would be unequalizing and the apparent antipoverty impact of the policies a mirage.

The point of this discussion is clear: A reliable evaluation of antipoverty tax–transfer programs must consider both the direct and the indirect redistributional effects of the policies. Consideration of only direct distributional effects may lead to a misestimation of how much an antipoverty tax–transfer policy helps the poor—or may fail to uncover the fact that the policy actually favors the rich.

The purpose of this study is to develop an empirical methodology by which to evaluate the full—direct plus indirect—effects of tax–transfer policy. A microeconomic simulation model is developed and used in analyzing the two tax–transfer programs described in this chapter. The model permits the indirect effects of the policy on the total distributional impact to be more fully understood. It is hoped that this or other models that consider both direct and indirect redistributional effects will be used increasingly in the evaluation of proposals for tax–transfer policy—supplanting the heavy reliance of previous evaluations on analysis of direct distributional effects only.

3

Modeling the microeconomic effects of tax—transfer policy: Conceptual issues

As emphasized in Chapter 1, the economic consequences of national income-support programs have been subject to substantial research and analysis. These research efforts have been motivated in large measure by the long-standing controversy regarding these consequences and by the political significance of various positions in this controversy. For example, research into the effects of income transfers on labor supply was motivated by the prevailing belief that large-scale cash transfers to individuals would cause a serious erosion of work incentives and a consequent reduction in work effort. Similarly, interest in the effects of transfers on fertility was stimulated by the belief that transfers would create artificial economic incentives for reproduction. In addition to such beliefs, which undermine the political viability of transfer programs, substantial uncertainty exists about the more general economic effects of such programs. It is not immediately obvious which income classes would ultimately gain or lose from such policy changes. Nor is it evident how consequent changes in consumption and production patterns would affect various regions, industries, or occupations. People are concerned not only with the direct benefits or the tax increases they will receive from such programs, but also with how the program-induced changes in the economic structure will affect their region of the country, the industry in which they work, or the labor market in which they operate.

In this chapter and the one following, we outline an empirical model that permits numerical analyses of these microeconomic effects of federal tax–transfer programs. The discussion in this chapter focuses on the structure of the model and the major conceptual issues that surround this structure. Chapter 4 describes the procedures followed in estimating the structure and indicates the modifications of the structure that were required to accommodate the constraints of data availability and computational feasibility.

Structure of the model

The model developed in this study treats a federal tax–transfer program as an exogenously imposed redistribution of disposable income from those families who bear the taxes that finance the program to those who receive benefits from it. The net beneficiaries will possess distinct tastes and needs and will be concentrated in particular geographic areas. If the policy has an antipoverty objective, these families will be concentrated at the lower end of the income distribution and in the poorer regions of the nation. Families that bear the cost of the program in the form of taxes will also have a distinct regional distribution and distinct tastes. If the program is financed by a progressive tax, these families will be concentrated at the upper end of the income distribution and in the richer regions of the nation.

Because program beneficiaries and cost bearers have different tastes, such a redistribution of income will affect both the level and the item composition of household expenditures. In response, there will be shifts in the location of both consumption and production and, in turn, changes in the derived demands for factor inputs. Identifying these induced changes in regional, industrial, and occupational patterns requires a model that captures the sequence of responses set into motion by the policy change. The level of empirical detail required by such a model exceeds the limits of analytic methods; hence, the empirical method we have constructed is a numerical simulation model.

The model is short-term in nature. It presumes that technology, the location of industries and households, and the structure of prices are fixed. Within this structure, it analyzes the consumption and production responses to short-run demand shifts initiated by a redistribution of income. These short-term effects, while clearly essential to political debate, cannot be readily analyzed by conventional comparative statics methods.

In order to focus on these short-term economic effects, the micro-simulation model developed portrays the economy by a set of causally ordered submodels (hereafter referred to as modules). These sequentially related modules capture the behavior of individuals or industries in response to changes in disposable incomes or in levels of demand for goods or services. Thus, the first module describes the effects on the distribution of disposable personal income of changes in federal tax or transfer policy. The second module depicts the responses of households to changes in disposable income, in terms of both item expenditures and total household expenditures. The third module represents the reactions of producers to the changes in levels and patterns of household demands. More specifically, it generates estimates of the changes in output, by industry and by region, required to satisfy increments in household demands. The fourth module portrays the shifts in factor requirements that result from induced changes in gross production. The fifth and final module assesses the distribution of incremental earned income resulting from changes in demand for workers of various earnings levels and simulates the distribution of incremental earned income among families of various income levels.

The structure of the model permits it to be operated recursively. In principle, one might revise preprogram incomes to reflect changes in earned incomes generated during the first period of analysis, then replay the model. In the present study, however, recursive operation has not been attempted. Because of the rather primitive assumptions regarding lag structure that would have had to be employed, the increment to the validity of estimates from recursive operation was judged to be minimal. Moreover, as the empirical analyses reported later reveal, the model is dynamically unstable; for longer-term analyses, explicit consideration of price changes would be necessary to insure valid estimates.

Finally, the model is demand led. The policy change is viewed as triggering a sequence of decisions implying a changed pattern of sectoral demands. The supply side of markets responds, at existing prices, to the changes in short-run demands. This procedure is implicit in the open Leontief system, an extended version of which forms one of the modules in the full model.[1]

In sum, then, the model developed in this study contains substan-

[1] Extensions of the Leontief system have proceeded in several directions in recent years. Examples of efforts to regionalize the system are Wassily W. Leontief et al., "The Economic Impact—Industrial and Regional—of an Arms Cut," *Review of Economics and Statistics* 47 (August 1965):217–241; Robert H. Haveman and John V. Krutilla, *Unemploy-*

tially more sectoral detail than do more standard empirical approaches to the estimation of the distributional effects of policy changes. Whereas the standard approaches typically employ reduced-form relationships among aggregate economic variables and income flows of various economic and demographic groups,[2] this model explicitly estimates induced patterns of consumer demand, the structure of interindustry relationships, and the detailed occupational and skill requirements implied by altered industry outputs. As a result, the indirect distributional consequences of the policy change can be compared with the direct consequences, and, more importantly, the income distribution created by the sum of direct and indirect distributional effects can be compared with the income distribution existing prior to the policy change.

Components of the model

The tax–transfer module

The problem of the tax–transfer module is to isolate the beneficiaries and cost bearers of public income-redistribution programs and to evaluate the gains and losses of each group. Several conceptual issues make this apparently straightforward task nontrivial.

The first critical issue in both the design and the evaluation of tax

Footnote 1 (*continued*)
ment, Excess Capacity, and the Evaluation of Public Expenditures: National and Regional Analyses (Baltimore: Johns Hopkins Press, 1969); William H. Miernyk et al., *Simulating Regional Economic Development* (Lexington, Mass.: Lexington Books, D. C. Heath, 1970); and Karen R. Polenske, *The United States Multiregional Input–Output Model* (Lexington, Mass.: Lexington Books, D. C. Heath, forthcoming). Extensions of the model to incorporate the occupational requirements implied by expansion of input–output sectors are presented in Haveman and Krutilla, *Evaluation of Public Expenditures;* Roger R. Bezdek, *Manpower Analysis Within an Interindustry Framework: Theoretical Potential and Empirical Problems,* Economic Research Group Working Paper no. 2, (Urbana, Ill.: Center for Advanced Computation, 1971); and Stephen P. Dresch and Robert D. Goldberg, "Research Methodology—IDIOM*: An Interindustry, National–Regional Policy Evaluation Model," *Annals of Economic and Social Measurement* 2 (1973):323–341.
[2]See Charles E. Metcalf, "The Size Distribution of Personal Income During the Business Cycle," *American Economic Review* 59 (September 1969):657–668; Edward C. Budd and David F. Seiders, "Micro Aspects of Macro Performance: The Impact of Inflation on the Distribution of Income and Wealth," *American Economic Review* 61 (May 1971):128–138; Thad W. Mirer, "The Distributional Impact of the 1970 Recession," *Review of Economics and Statistics* 55 (May 1973):214–224; and Edward M. Gramlich, "The Distributional Effects of Higher Unemployment," *Brookings Papers on Economic Activity,* no. 2 (1974), pp. 293–336.

or transfer proposals arises from the transitory nature of observed income flows.[3] In the design of income-transfer programs, this issue is confronted in the choice of the accounting period on which to base benefit payments. Short accounting periods favor those individuals with seasonal or irregular income flows—enabling them to qualify for benefits during a year even though their annual incomes exceed the eligibility level—and create incentives to bunch income.

In evaluations of a program's distributional impact on various households, this transitory-income phenomenon is reflected in the problem of choosing the measure of economic status to be employed in the analysis. The distributional patterns estimated are likely to be highly dependent on the measure of economic status, or well-being, chosen. For example, if economic status is measured by permanent income, the creation of an antipoverty transfer program will be said to increase the well-being of a family with low permanent income—even though in any given year the family's observed income may be sufficiently high to make it ineligible for benefits. The family's permanent income will rise because of the program, even if its observed income in a specific year remains unaffected. Conversely, if well-being is measured by annual income, a family with high permanent income may be a major beneficiary in a given year if, for transitory reasons, its income that year is below the eligibility level. The annual disposable income of the household may rise while its permanent income is unchanged.

This transitory-income problem, then, makes critical the choice of an income base on which to estimate program effects. Because the purpose of this analysis is to evaluate behavioral responses, the nature of the behavior to be evaluated will influence this choice.

A second issue is also related to the transitory-income phenomenon. The structure of many income-conditioned tax or transfer programs reduces the variance in the distribution of covered households' disposable income flows. For example, a progressive income tax absorbs a relatively high proportion of transitorily high income flows.

---

[3]The transitory nature of pretax, pretransfer household income has been analyzed in Terence F. Kelly, "Factors Affecting Poverty: A Gross Flow Analysis," in U.S. President, Commission on Income Maintenance Programs, *Technical Studies* (Washington, D.C.: U.S. Government Printing Office, 1970), pp. 1–3, (Pr 36.8: In 2/T22); Thad Mirer, "Aspects of the Variability of Family Income," in *Five Thousand American Families—Patterns of Economic Progress*, vol. 2, ed. James N. Morgan (Ann Arbor: University of Michigan, Institute for Social Research, Survey Research Center, 1974), pp. 201–211; and James N. Morgan et al., *Five Thousand American Families—Patterns of Economic Progress*, vol. 1 (Ann Arbor: University of Michigan, Institute for Social Research, Survey Research Center, 1974).

Similarly, cash-transfer programs for the poor truncate the distribution of annual income by providing some minimum income guarantee. If the degree of uncertainty regarding future income flows is a component of household well-being, the creation of income-conditioned tax or transfer programs will increase household well-being by reducing this uncertainty. Moreover, the increase in well-being will be larger for those units with high transitory components to income flows than for households with stable income patterns. Attempts to evaluate the distribution of real benefits and losses from any tax or transfer program should distinguish, at least in concept, between households with high and low transitory components to income flows.

Finally, no matter what indicator of economic status is employed—whether current or permanent income—the accuracy of estimates of distributional impacts depends on households' behavioral responses to the program. For example, if the availability of transfer benefits results in reduced labor supply and reduced household earnings, estimates of program benefits based on levels of household income *prior to* the program will be biased downward. Again, accurate evaluation of the distribution of tax or transfer benefits and losses must incorporate these behavioral responses.

In the tax–transfer simulation module employed in this study, program effects are estimated on the basis of both current income and permanent (or normal) income, to provide boundary estimates of the effect of the program on household well-being. However, the differential effect of reduction of uncertainty for households with varying transitory components of income is ignored, as are induced effects on labor supply. The procedure employed requires information on household attributes that condition transfer benefits and tax costs (income of various types, family size, deductions, and so on), and yields estimates of benefits and losses to households of various categories.

The consumption expenditure module

The second module simulates the expenditure responses of households to changes in disposable income resulting from taxes or transfers. The analysis proceeds in two steps: First, the change in aggregate household expenditures is estimated, and second, the item composition of the marginal expenditure is examined.

As with the tax–transfer module, transitory income flows pose the most serious conceptual problem in the development of this module. As emphasized earlier, a change in tax or transfer policy may affect both household disposable income in any particular year and the level of household permanent income. The alterations in current and permanent income need not be of the same magnitude nor, indeed, of the same sign. To the extent that changes in tax–transfer policy represent permanent changes in the income-generation process, any household that anticipates future income levels that will qualify it for either program benefits or tax costs will experience a change in its permanent income. As indicated earlier, the policy will affect permanent income of households both by altering the expected level of income flows (due to expected taxes or transfers) and by reducing the variance in the distribution of disposable income. Transitory phenomena, however, may cause the change in actual disposable income in any year resulting from taxes or transfers to be more or less than the permanent change.

The objective of this module is to evaluate the effect on consumption expenditures of increments in disposable income. If the change in current disposable income is considered a reliable predictor of the changes in consumption and savings, the policy's effect on the level of household permanent income can be neglected for the purpose of this module. However, if changes in savings and consumption depend primarily on changes in household permanent income, this variable must be estimated.

Unfortunately, although substantial research on consumption behavior has been undertaken, the controversy over the determinants of consumption expenditures remains unresolved. While economic theory suggests that permanent income is the primary determinant of consumption and savings,[4] only current income is observable. Moreover, empirical analyses provide as much support for the hypothesis that marginal consumption patterns depend on changes in current income as for the hypothesis that they depend on changes in permanent income.[5]

[4]See Milton Friedman, *A Theory of the Consumption Function*, A Study by the National Bureau of Economic Research, New York (Princeton: Princeton University Press, 1957). See also Franco Modigliani and Albert Ando, "The 'Permanent Income' and the 'Life Cycle' Hypothesis of Saving Behavior: Comparison and Tests," in *Proceedings of the Conference on Consumption and Saving*, vol. 2, ed. Irwin Friend and Robert Jones (Philadelphia: University of Pennsylvania, 1960), pp. 49–174; Franco Modigliani and Richard Blumberg, "Utility Analysis and the Consumption Function: An Interpretation of Cross-Section Data," in *Post-Keynesian Economics*, ed. Kenneth K. Kurihara (London: George Allen and Unwin, 1955), pp. 388–436; and Albert Ando and Franco Modigliani, "The 'Life Cycle' Hypothesis of Saving: Aggregate Implications and Tests," *American Economic Review* 53 (March 1963):55–84.

[5]For a review of the extensive empirical analysis of the relationship between household expenditures and changes in both current and permanent income, see Robert

A second problem in constructing this module results from the discrepancy between the notions of consumption and current expenditures. This problem is most serious for households with a high transitory component of income—especially the transitorily poor. By drawing down stocks of durable and semidurable goods (primarily clothing, furniture, appliances, and automobiles), this group may be able to maintain a level of real consumption above that implied by their level of current income. Moreover, to the extent that liquid assets are available to this group, current *expenditures* may be greater than the level predicted by current income—and, indeed, may actually exceed current income. This problem is as acute for estimating the composition of consumption or consumption expenditures as it is for estimating the level of these flows.

Specification of a consumption expenditure module that resolves all these issues is impossible. Instead, alternative methods of estimating expenditures have been developed. These methods differ in their portrayals of the impact of current taxes or transfers on the level of consumption expenditures and in their representations of the determinants of the pattern of item expenditures. They respond, albeit imperfectly, to the difficulty of estimating household permanent income, to the absence of an adequate stock-adjustment model for consumer durables, and to the impossibility of identifying households whose long-term economic status will be influenced by the program but whose *current* economic status is unaffected. Each of the approaches seeks to capture some aspect of the household expenditure process emphasized in the theory of consumer behavior. In this sense, the empirical estimates they generate can be viewed as bounds of the response of expenditure levels and composition to changes in tax–transfer policy.

The gross output module

This module is designed to trace the indirect, interindustry output changes generated by the changes in the level, the commodity pattern, and the regional pattern of household expenditures estimated in the

Footnote 5 (*continued*)
Ferber, "Research on Household Behavior," *American Economic Review* 52 (March 1962):19–63.

The discrepancy between the effects of a tax–transfer scheme on current income and normal income have been noted in the literature. For example, Moeller, in his study of expenditure responses to a negative income tax, reported budget shares based upon measures of both current income and permanent income—as proxied by total expenditure. See John F. Moeller, "Household Budget Responses to Negative Income Tax Simulations" (Ph.D. dissertation, University of Wisconsin–Madison, 1970).

previous module. A detailed characterization of production by sector and region is maintained to permit analysis of spatial effects as well as of impacts on particular markets.

In principle, analysis of adjustments to increased demand for particular commodities involves minimizing the costs of production, given prices of inputs and a production function. Short-term adjustments, by definition, preclude modification of the stock of capital, thereby profoundly limiting the opportunities for factor substitution. Here a simple linear technology is postulated. This step clearly incorporates the theoretically limited assumption that marginal and average input requirements are identical. In the short run, this is probably not an unrealistic assertion when applied to intermediate inputs; it is less acceptable when applied to primary factors—labor and capital. Furthermore, as subsequent chapters will reveal, the increase in output for any sector, even within detailed regions, is modest, a finding that reduces the seriousness of the assumption of linearity.

To estimate direct and indirect regional output responses, a Leontief model of production[6] is postulated for each region. The regions are then joined by a fixed-coefficients trading model. The production and factor-use adjustments of producers to changes in expenditures induced by the tax–transfer policy are assumed to occur within the period. Through this procedure, the module incorporates the simplifying assumptions of a Leontief technology—linearity, additivity, and nonsubstitutability. In addition, it presumes that trading patterns are fixed and that they are invariant within a sector, regardless of whether a commodity is used as a final good by households or as an input into further production.

The factor employment module

Employing estimates of the shifts in regional and sectoral production from the previous module, this fourth module appraises the changes in factor demands resulting from incremental production. The sectoral and regional detail of the gross output module is maintained and is supplemented by substantial occupational detail.

In principle, the demand for labor inputs might be derived from analyses of short-run production functions for each sector. It is expected that increases in demand for outputs will be met by more intensive use of capital and overhead labor and by roughly proportional increases in

[6]See Wassily W. Leontief et al., *Studies in the Structure of the American Economy* (New York: Oxford University Press, 1953) for an early description of the structure of this model.

demand for directly productive inputs—production workers and materials. If the shift in production rates is perceived to be permanent, producers will be expected to adapt their plants over time to the long-run equilibrium technology, but this process will be time consuming. Similarly, the short-term and long-term responses of factor suppliers should also differ. In the very short run, restoration of full-time or overtime employment may be used to meet production requirements. In the long run, supplies of labor will be expected to adapt, and equilibrium wages may rise.

Modeling these phenomena, while conceptually straightforward, carries overwhelming empirical requirements. Hence, the model of the factor market employed in this module is much simpler than a fully specified model. This model relies on fixed-coefficients production functions in identifying derived factor demands. In effect, it extends the assumptions of the Leontief system to the demand for factor inputs. Because it is a short-term model, the assumption of nonsubstitutability is not unreasonable; changes in factor proportions for any sector require replacement or modernization of vintage capital stocks, a time-consuming activity. In addition, the model assumes that factor markets clear instantaneously with no changes in factor prices. This assumption implicitly requires infinitely elastic factor supply functions in all markets. Given the relatively small shifts in factor demands generated by the empirical model, this requirement also seems reasonable.[7] Through this module, then, gross output changes in production sectors by region are translated into changes in factor employment by occupational category, by production sector, and again by region.[8]

The income distribution module

This final module evaluates the impact of program-stimulated production and employment on the size distribution of income. In order

---

[7] If larger-scale programs or programs with more focused effects were being analyzed, a more explicit model of the factor market would be required. It should be noted that such small changes in demands within markets minimize the importance of the Leontief assumptions in the gross output module, since they mean that the probable changes in the relative prices of factors will be trivial and hence not affect input proportions even if production functions exhibit continuous substitutability.

[8] In the empirical model, only the effects of demand changes on labor employment are evaluated. As will be noted in Chapter 4, the reliability of capital coefficients in such a short-term model, together with the difficulty of tracing the incidence of incremental changes in capital use, argue against the empirical modeling of this effect on factor employment.

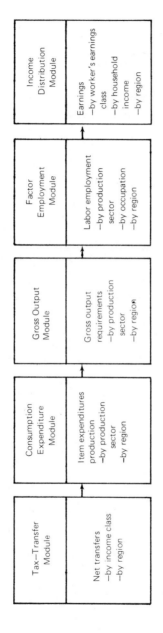

FIGURE 3.1. Causal structure of the model.

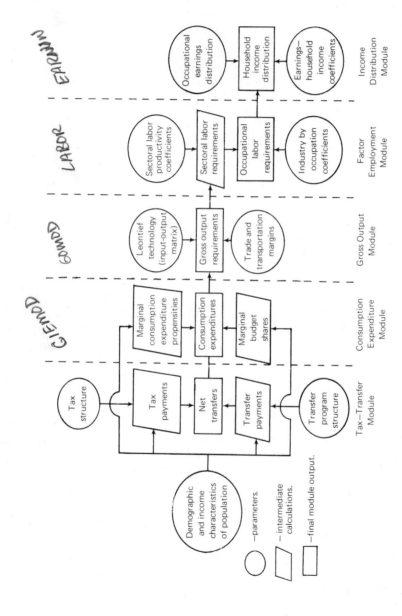

FIGURE 3.2. Data and parameter structure of the model.

24

to specify the distributional component of the changes in factor employment, additional assumptions regarding the operation of factor markets
are required.[9] First, it is assumed that the distribution of earned income
for those employed in an occupation in a region reflects the distribution
of skill, ability, and work effort of workers in that occupation and region.
Hence, the distribution by skill, ability, and work effort of any induced
employment in that occupation and region is taken to be the same as the
distribution of existing employment. This fixed-pattern approach to
assigning increases and decreases in earnings permits estimation of the
distribution of increments to earned income by earnings class for each
region. As a second step, earnings changes for individual workers
grouped by earnings class are mapped into households grouped by income class. This transformation, employing fixed ratios describing the
relationship of individual earnings to household income, yields estimates of the changes in household income generated by the change in
tax—transfer policy. In this transformation from earnings by earnings
class of worker to earnings by income class of household, it is assumed
that the policy-induced increment to earnings in a regional earnings
class is divided equally among the members of that earnings class.

The complete simulation model is summarized in Figures 3.1 and
3.2. In Figure 3.1 the causal structure of the model is displayed in sche-
matic form. The figure identifies the modules that describe the sequence
of choices provoked by a shift in tax—transfer policy. Figure 3.2 provides
a more detailed statement of the data and parameter requirements of
each module and its outputs. The formal relationships between modules
are suggested by the arrows indicating the use of the results of a previous module as data input into the subsequent module.

---

[9]Because only effects on labor employment are modeled in the factor employment
module, the distributional discussion in this section is in terms of the labor market.

4

Modeling the microeconomic effects of tax—transfer policy: Empirical issues

In order to estimate the parameters of the sequential simulation model described in Chapter 3, diverse sources of data are required. The limitations of available data necessitate a number of simplifications and analytic compromises. In this chapter we discuss the data used in the study, the procedures employed in estimating parameters, and the simplifications adopted to meet data and computational constraints. Also, we examine the implications of these simplifications for the interpretation of empirical results.

Empirical implementation of the model

The tax—transfer module

The first module simulates the impact on household income of the specific changes in tax—transfer policy described in Chapter 2. It first estimates the total cost of the transfer programs and the distribution of benefits by type of household, then estimates the distribution of a proportional increase in the federal personal income tax to cover the costs of the transfer program. The surtax is specified as a constant percentage of preprogram income-tax liabilities. In estimating the distribution of both transfers and taxes, program rules are applied to a sample survey of households.

The tax–transfer module relies on the Current Population Survey (CPS) as the primary data file.[1] The CPS is an annual, national survey undertaken by the U.S. Bureau of the Census that includes detailed information on demographic and socioeconomic characteristics, and on family and individual income by source, for approximately 50,000 American households. The empirical experiments reported in this monograph are based on the March 1971 survey's income data for the calendar year 1970, adjusted to reflect the characteristics of the 1973 population. The adjustments allow for demographic changes, economic growth, inflation, and changes in the unemployment rate. The microsimulation of population change is based on the modeling efforts of the Urban Institute's Transfer Income Program Evaluation Project.[2]

Demographic changes during the period 1970–1973 are approximated by a crude simulation technique. The sample weighting factors for observations in the 1971 CPS are adjusted to reflect changes in total population, family dissolution and formation, family size, and headship. These adjustments are accomplished by aging each survey cell weight by a factor representing the geometric mean rate of change in size of the population represented by the cell.[3] The rates are obtained by analyzing trends from 1966 to 1970. Thus the demographic simulation represents a transformation of the sample survey under the assumption

[1] See U.S. Bureau of the Census, Current Population Reports, series P-60, Consumer Income (Washington, D.C.: U.S. Government Printing Office, 1948–1975) (C56.218:P-60/), for a detailed description of the survey and analyses of the data generated by it.

[2] See Nelson McClung, John Moeller, and Eduardo Siguel, "Transfer Income Program Evaluation," Urban Institute Working Paper 950-3 (Washington, D.C., 1971). This report provides detailed discussion of the computational aspects of the adjustments.

[3] These adjustment factors were estimated from the historical series reported in U.S. Bureau of the Census, "Projections of the Population of the United States by Age, Sex, and Color to 1990, with Extensions of Population by Age and Sex to 2015," Current Population Reports, series P-25, Population Estimates and Projections, no. 381 (Washington, D.C.: U.S. Government Printing Office, 1967) (C3.186:P-25/381); U.S. Bureau of the Census, "Summary of Demographic Projections," Current Population Reports, series P-25, Population Estimates and Projections, no. 388 (Washington, D.C.: U.S. Government Printing Office, 1968) (C3.186:P-25/388); and U.S. Bureau of the Census, "Projections of the Population of the United States, by Age and Sex (Interim Revisions): 1970 to 2020," Current Population Reports, series P-25, Population Estimates and Projections, no. 448 (Washington, D.C.: U.S. Government Printing Office, 1970) (C3.186:P-25/448).

that previous trends in the characteristics of households were maintained over the three-year period 1970–1973.

Inflation and productivity growth are expected to increase both the nominal and the real incomes of households. Since program benefits are conditioned upon current nominal income, these values are important. A procedure analogous to that used in projecting demographic trends is employed to adjust for inflation and productivity growth. Geometric growth rates of nominal incomes are applied to incomes reported for 1970. These growth rates are based on recent experience and are specific to the detailed sources of earned and unearned income reported in the CPS.

An unemployment rate corresponding to actual experience during the survey period is implied by the data. For the survey year, 1970, this rate was 6.0 percent. In order to permit parametric evaluation within the module of the effects of alternate unemployment rates, a simulation of unemployment experiences is introduced. This submodule randomly assigns unemployment and duration of unemployment to groups identified by age, sex, occupation, and unemployment experience. Three broad populations are considered—new workers, currently unemployed persons, and currently employed persons.

Data for the period 1964–1966 indicate that a 1.00 percent increase in unemployment implies that an additional 2.16 percent of the labor force will incur some period of unemployment during the year. This increment (or decrement) to unemployment is distributed across occupations according to the ratio of employment in each occupation to total employment. Thus, the change in unemployment experienced by individuals as unemployment rates change is assumed to be distributed uniformly over occupations. However, the *duration* of an event of unemployment is determined separately. Duration of unemployment, in weeks, is assigned stochastically to each member of the labor force; the underlying probabilities are specified to be conditional upon sex and age, with the new entrant to the labor force being in a distinct "age" group. Each worker's earnings are decreased by the product of normal weekly earnings (from the CPS) and weeks unemployed.

For those workers reported in the survey as unemployed, it is only necessary to assign estimates of duration of unemployment and to evaluate their Unemployment Compensation benefits. The procedure for assigning duration is identical to that described above. Reported duration to date is subtracted from estimated duration; where the result is negative, the duration is assumed to be zero. In the simulations reported in this monograph an unemployment rate of 4.9 percent is chosen.

Errors in the data. The CPS contains acknowledged errors that make it necessary to edit the data files in order to eliminate or mitigate problems that would directly affect simulation results. Problems result from respondent errors, interviewer errors, and transcription and coding errors. To identify them, two levels of consistency checks are introduced. First, a set of internal consistency checks for the joint occurrence of events is employed. Records that violate any of these checks are manually evaluated and, if possible, corrected. Second, a set of external consistency checks is applied to the CPS data.

The internal checks test for logically inconsistent responses, as follows:

1. The sum of income from all sources should equal total family income.
2. The sum of individual incomes for all members of the household should also equal family income.
3. Weeks worked in previous year (estimated by dividing previous year's total earned income by previous week's earned income) should approximate reported weeks worked.
4. The product of reported weeks worked in previous year and earnings in previous week should approximate reported earnings for previous year.

For households not responding to items on the CPS, imputations are made based on the responses of similar households. That is, cell means for detailed attributes are assigned to nonrespondents.

External consistency checks based on control totals derived from other data sets are also applied to the CPS estimates of population attributes. Wherever there is a clear presumption that the controls are more reliable, discrepancies are distributed proportionally over the smallest relevant subgroup. The 1970 U.S. Census of Population, the Brookings Institution's edited Survey of Economic Opportunity (SEO) file, and Internal Revenue Service income statistics[4] are sources of benchmarks.

Disaggregation. In addition to the problems noted above, several difficulties stem from differences between the CPS and the transfer proposal in the dimensionality or definitions of variables. One problem arises in connection with how to treat receipts from other transfer programs in determining the size of proposed transfer payments. The

---

[4]U.S. Department of the Treasury, Internal Revenue Service, *Statistics of Income: 1970, Individual Income Tax Returns,* publication 79 (10-72) (Washington, D.C.: Department of the Treasury, 1972) (T22.35/2:In2/970).

problem is that the CPS reports transfer receipts as a unit, while the transfer proposals distinguish between veterans' benefits, Aid to the Blind, public assistance, and Old Age, Survivors, Disability, and Health Insurance.

A more serious discrepancy occurs between the accounting periods used in the CPS and those used for calculating transfer payments. To deal with this discrepancy, it is necessary to convert the CPS data on annual income into figures on weekly income. Reported earned income is divided by reported weeks worked. This procedure yields average weekly income, which is then multiplied by estimated weeks worked per accounting period to obtain an income estimate that can be used for the means test.

The tax–transfer module applies the statutory rules of the transfer and tax schemes to the edited and adjusted sample of households, then applies adjusted weighting factors to the sample observations to obtain estimates of national and regional benefit and cost distributions. The target yield of the revenue package is set equal to the estimated cost of the transfer program. Because a surtax on the federal personal income tax has been specified as the financing mechanism in these experiments, the distribution of the burden of the federal personal income tax is simulated first, and then a surtax rate that assures the target yield is applied.

This module yields estimates of the total cost of the transfer scheme, the distribution of transfer receipts by detailed demographic and economic characteristics of households, the rate of surtax necessary to finance the scheme, and the distribution of tax liabilities by type of household. In addition, the module identifies the regions of residence of both transfer beneficiaries and taxpayers.

The consumption expenditure module

The second module simulates the expenditure responses of households to changes in income resulting from changes in tax or transfer policy. In order to deal with unresolvable conceptual problems in the empirical analysis of consumption expenditures, this module incorporates three alternative methods of estimating expenditures. The first method reflects the view that changes in current disposable income cause changes in the level and composition of consumption expenditures. The second and third methods presume instead that changes in consumption expenditure levels and patterns result from changes in normal income. Each of these methods applies empirical estimates of marginal savings rates to increments or decrements of income and distributes the resulting expenditure change among items according to estimated vectors of marginal budget shares. In each case, the effects of family size, age of head, tenure, education, and race are recognized in determining incremental expenditure levels and patterns.

The use of alternative estimating methods encompassing both the current-income and the normal-income views of expenditure behavior is appropriate, given the permanent alteration in the nation's income-generation process that would be created by the policy changes under consideration. The new policies would alter both the current income of households eligible for benefits or incurring tax liabilities and the normal income of households expecting to be benefit recipients or cost bearers at some future date. As noted in Chapter 3, such permanent changes in the tax–transfer system would appear to certain groups (such as the permanently poor) to be continuously available and, hence, to produce a similar change in both current income and normal income. However, other groups (the relatively affluent) would regard the transfer policy as a cushion during a temporary reversal, affecting normal income only marginally; they would consume at approximately their preprogram level during such a reversal, through depleting durable assets, dissaving, and using current transfer receipts. Consequently, the patterns of expenditures by the temporarily poor and by the permanently poor are likely to respond quite differently to such a policy change. While the three methods of estimating expenditures developed here do not resolve this conceptual problem, they do give partial recognition to the different behavioral responses predicted by the current-income and normal-income views of consumption behavior.

The principal data base used in all versions of the expenditure module is the 1960–1961 Consumer Expenditure Survey (CES) conducted by the U.S. Department of Labor.[5] The data file from this survey contains usable, detailed commodity expenditure records for 13,728 consumer units. While this is an enormously rich body of expenditure data, it is less than ideal for the purposes of this study, for several reasons. First, the survey is somewhat outdated. Use of expenditure patterns observed in 1959 for estimating 1973 behavior requires assuming that, in the intervening period, tastes have not changed, the characteristics of commodities within each category have remained constant, and relative prices have not changed significantly. Second, a large number of household characteristics believed to be associated with normal income—and

---

[5] For a complete description of these data, see U.S. Department of Labor, Bureau of Labor Statistics, *Consumer Expenditures and Income: Survey Guidelines*, bulletin 1684 (Washington, D.C.: U.S. Government Printing Office, 1971) (L2.3:1684).

hence important to the estimating methods that base expenditures on normal income—were not covered by the survey. Finally, because the data refer to household expenditures rather than to consumption, no recognition can be given to the difference between expenditures on durable goods and the consumption of their service flows.

Method 1. The first method of estimating expenditures assumes that changes in current income in any given year from tax liabilities or transfer receipts motivate changes in consumption expenditures in that year. Marginal expenditure propensities and marginal budget shares are estimated from cross-sectional expenditure models applied to survey data on household expenditures. These parameters are then applied to policy-induced changes in current income of households stratified by income class and region, to yield an allocation of expenditure changes among commodity categories and regions. Seven income classes, 23 regions, and 56 commodity categories are employed.

Because of the permanent change in the income-generation process—and the implied alteration of the underlying structure determining savings behavior—that the policy change would cause, reasonable marginal expenditure propensities were adopted in place of the econometric estimates of propensities based on observations reflecting the preprogram structure. The point of departure in determining these parameters was a study by Irwin Friend and Stanley Schor.[6] The seven income classes employed in the simulations and their marginal expenditure propensities are shown in Table 4.1.

The values in the table represent the ratios of the increments in household expenditures to increments in income within income classes. Household expenditures are defined as current consumption expenditures plus gifts and contributions, and income is defined as money income after taxes minus account balancing differences. Friend and Schor found that the empirical marginal propensity to spend of the lowest-income group was .52. This unusually low value resulted from the presence in this group of large numbers of temporarily poor households who apparently rely heavily on accumulated assets during periods of financial reversal. Since an income-maintenance scheme would eliminate the possibility of such very low incomes, these empirical estimates appear to be inappropriate for the present study. Therefore, the

[6]Irwin Friend and Stanley Schor, "Who Saves?" in *Proceedings of the Conference on Consumption and Saving,* vol. 2, ed. Irwin Friend and Robert Jones (Philadelphia: University of Pennsylvania, 1960), pp. 223–296. These estimates are based on the 1960–1961 Survey of Consumer Expenditures.

TABLE 4.1

Marginal propensities to spend, by income class

Preprogram income class (1960–1961 dollars)	Marginal propensity to spend
$1477 or less	1.09
$1478–$2216	1.09
$2217–$2955	1.01
$2956–$3694	.89
$3695–$4432	.84
$4433–$8865	.70
$8866 or more	.57

empirical estimate for the lowest-income group has been replaced by a more likely estimate that preserves monotonicity in the relationship between income and expenditures. In applying these propensities to program-induced income changes, adjustments are made for price changes between 1960–1961 (the effective date of the Friend–Schor estimates) and 1973. Families whose income is changed by the program are assigned marginal expenditure propensities on the basis of their pre-program income class, a procedure that results in some upward bias in the expenditure estimates. These propensities are not differentiated by region.

Vectors of marginal budget shares are obtained from a piecewise log linear regression analysis in which household expenditures on each of 56 commodities are regressed against family income, family size, education of head, home ownership, region, age of head, and urban–rural location.[7] The estimated income coefficients indicate the change in

---

[7]The specification of the regression model was chosen to accomodate non-linearities observed in previous studies and was patterned after that developed by John F. Moeller in his study of expenditure response to income-transfer policies. See John F. Moeller, "Household Budget Responses to Negative Income Tax Simulations" (Ph.D. dissertation, University of Wisconsin–Madison, 1970). A detailed description of the derivation of these marginal budget shares is presented in Appendix D.

Income data from the 1960–1961 Consumer Expenditure Survey (CES) were inflated to 1973 values through the use of the GNP deflator. The expenditure data for each household provide a detailed breakdown of total consumption into 343 categories, a small number of which are catchall and residual categories. These detailed expenditure categories were regrouped into 56 categories that coincide with the sectors delivering goods to households for final use. The mapping rules were developed for a matching of Standard Industrial Classification (SIC) codes to the Multiregional Input–Output Model (MRIO) input–output sectors and the items reported in the CES. This mapping was later modified in some details to correspond more nearly to the rules adopted by the MRIO

expenditures on any commodity—the marginal propensity to purchase that commodity—in response to a change in household income for that income class, controlling for other social and demographic variables that are expected to affect commodity expenditures. To transform these vectors of marginal propensity into a vector of marginal budget shares, the total of marginal propensities for all commodities for each income class is divided into each element in the vector, yielding a vector of budget shares the sum of whose elements is, by construction, unity.

The separation of savings behavior from patterns of item expenditures is motivated by the judgment that savings propensities under a reformed transfer scheme are more likely than patterns of expenditures to be misrepresented by the empirical estimates of expenditures. By separating these two sets of parameters it is possible to observe explicitly the empirical consequences of experimentally manipulating the savings propensities.

Methods 2 and 3. The second and third methods of estimating expenditures reflect the notion that expenditure levels and patterns respond to changes in normal income. To approximate normal income, households are grouped by characteristics thought to determine income potential—age, occupation, and race. A total of 177 groupings is employed.[8] The mean income of the households in a cell is assumed to equal the normal income of each household in the cell. Any deviation of current household income from the estimated normal income is interpreted as a chance variation, which might be recognized by households in evaluating their normal income level. Thus, transfer benefits and tax liabilities in any given year reflect the variability of current income. For households in any cell, the mean transfer payment (or tax liability) of the cell is taken to be the change in normal income attributable to the program. While these estimates of normal income and program-induced changes in it are crude, they do capture several of the determinants of normal income. The limitations of the definition of normal income must be recognized in interpreting the consumption changes estimated by this model.

Footnote 7 (*continued*)
project as presented in Karen R. Polenske et al., "Appendix B: Alignment of 1960 Consumer Expenditures Survey Categories with the 80 Order Input–Output Industrial Classification," in *State Estimates of the Gross National Product, 1947, 1958, 1963,* by Karen R. Polenske et al. (Lexington, Mass.: Lexington Books, D.C. Heath, 1972), pp. 173–211. A detailed description of this alignment is presented in Appendix E.

[8] The attributes and statistical properties of the groups are shown in Appendix F.

In the second method of estimating expenditures, the propensity to spend out of changes in imputed normal income is determined by calculating the ratio of a cell's reported mean expenditure to its estimated normal income. Applying this ratio to the change in normal income attributable to the policy yields an estimate of the induced change in household expenditures.

The budget shares for each of the 177 normal-income cells are taken to be the percentage allocation of total expenditures among 56 commodities within each cell.[9] By applying these budget shares to the estimated change in household expenditures attributable to the program, estimates of expenditure responses for each commodity are obtained for each household.[10]

The third method of estimating expenditures combines features of the first two. As in the second method, changes in normal income are presumed to motivate changes in household expenditures. But estimates

---

[9]Implicit in this procedure is the assumption that the elasticity of demand with respect to normal income is unity for each commodity. For a typical family in cell j, let

E_i^j = total expenditure on commodity i;

Y_i^j = normal income;

E_i^j = elasticity of demand with respect to income.

By definition,

$$(1) \qquad E_i^j = \frac{\Delta E_i^j}{E_i^j} \cdot \frac{Y^j}{\Delta Y^j}.$$

But, by assumption,

$$(2) \qquad \frac{\Delta E_i^j}{\Delta Y^j} = \frac{E_i^j}{Y^j} \qquad \text{for all } j.$$

Therefore, substituting (2) into (1), we find

$$(3) \qquad E_i^j = 1 \text{ for all } j.$$

Hence, this procedure tends to bias upward (downward) expenditures on commodities with a low (high) elasticity of demand with respect to normal income.

[10]In the simulation exercises reported in this monograph, the estimated policy-induced change in normal income was obtained from Current Population Survey household data grouped into the 177 normal-income cells. The expenditure propensities and budget shares were obtained from household data in the Consumer Expenditure Survey, grouped into the same 177 normal-income cells.

TABLE 4.2
Three alternative methods of estimating consumption expenditures

	Change in household income	Change in household expenditures	Commodity composition of expenditure change
Method 1	Simulated household benefits and liabilities (from Tax–Transfer Module)	Income-class-specific marginal propensity to spend applied to change in household income	Estimated income-class-specific marginal budget shares applied to change in household expenditures
Method 2	Average benefits or liabilities of normal-income class of household	Average propensity to spend of normal-income class applied to change in household income	Budget shares of normal-income class applied to change in household expenditures
Method 3	Same as 2	Same as 1	Same as 1

of marginal savings propensities and marginal budget shares from the first method are employed to describe these changes.[11] These parameters, it will be recalled, relate incremental expenditure responses to current income.

The three expenditure-estimating methods are summarized in Table 4.2. As the table indicates, Method 1 follows a format based on current income and marginal expenditures throughout, while Method 2 adopts a rigid format based on normal income and average expenditures. Method 3 follows the normal-income strategy in estimating the policy-induced change in household income but transforms that income change into commodity expenditures via a procedure based on marginal expenditures and marginal budget shares. Although Method 1 follows the most straightforward and intuitive approach to analyzing consumption responses, it incorporates the assumption that benefit receipts will induce identical expenditure responses regardless of their transitory or permanent character. While Method 2 distinguishes between permanent and transitory benefits, it suffers from the unrealistic assumption that marginal response equals average response. Because of this assumption, Method 2 will underestimate the induced demands for commodities with high income elasticities and overestimate those with

[11] As noted earlier, available data do not permit calculation of marginal responses to changes in imputed normal income.

low income elasticities. While Method 3 distinguishes between per-manent and transitory impacts, it employs estimates of marginal re-sponses to changes in current income. As a result, for most commodities, expenditure estimates obtained by Method 3 will fall between those obtained by Method 1 and those obtained by Method 2.

The gross output module

Changes in the item expenditures of households may be summed to produce estimates of the shift in commodity demands by region. The gross output module analyzes the indirect, interindustry effects of changes in the pattern of household purchases by commodity and region. These gross production implications are estimated using a large-scale multiregional input–output system that portrays the national econ-omy as 79 sectors employing fixed-coefficient technologies unique to each of 23 regions.[12] Trading patterns are represented by fixed coeffi-cients that presume that any commodity in any particular region is sup-plied in fixed proportions by shipping regions. By multiplying regional increments to household expenditures by the appropriate form of this input–output matrix, the induced gross outputs of each of the 79 indus-tries in each of the 23 regions are estimated. These estimates by detailed industry and region are then presented.

Our interest in the indirect effects on production of a change in tax–transfer policy has three origins. First, the changes in demand for final goods approximate only crudely the impact of the policy on specific product markets. As the structure of production shifts, price adjustments and short-run supply bottlenecks are to be anticipated. These effects are of interest in their own right and also because of their potential impact—adverse or beneficial—on the population group the policy change is designed to help. To evaluate these effects, the impact of increased demands on industries supplying intermediate goods must also be analyzed. It is possible, for example, that an industry supplying a semifinished good or service may experience a greater production impact than any of the industries delivering goods or services directly to consumers. Similarly, prevailing interregional trading patterns may concentrate increased requirements for intermediate goods in limited regional markets.

[12]The 79 production sectors are listed in Appendix G. In Appendix H, the 23 regions are defined and the justification for this particular regional constellation is presented.

The second reason for interest in indirect effects on production concerns opportunities for regional economic development. To the extent that households that receive increases in disposable income demand items produced by industries located in relatively developed industrial areas, the indirect effect of the policy change will be to stimulate the more prosperous local economies. On the other hand, if the increased demand falls on industries concentrated in relatively less developed areas, the effect will be to stimulate the economies of these lower-income regions.

Finally, the simulation of indirect impacts on production is of interest as an intermediate step in evaluation of the effect of the program on earned incomes and, hence, of the ultimate costs of the program. The empirical results of this module, as described later, are primary inputs into a subsequent module designed to estimate the program's effect on the pattern of demands for and income to the primary factor inputs.

To estimate the direct and indirect regional output responses, a Leontief[13] model of production—incorporating the assumptions of linearity, additivity, and nonsubstitutability—is postulated for each region. The regions are then joined by a fixed-coefficients trading model, which asserts that regional trading patterns are invariant within a sector regardless of whether a commodity is used for final, household consumption, for input into further production, or for capital formation. Producers' adjustments of production and factor use in response to expenditure changes induced by tax–transfer policy are assumed to occur within the period. Moreover, the changes in earned income occasioned by these adjustments are assumed to have no first-period

---

[13] See Wassily W. Leontief et al., *Studies in the Structure of the American Economy* (New York: Oxford University Press, 1953) for an early description of the structure of this model. The primary features of this production technology are as follows:

1. Each productive activity has constant returns to scale; if output is doubled, then inputs must be doubled.
2. Marginal outputs from any sector require the same relative composition of inputs as does the total output of that sector; that is, each sector has fixed technical coefficients.
3. The economy is assumed to fully adjust within any stipulated period of time: say, one year. Thus, if a final demand of the size and composition of the annual Gross National Product is imposed on the model, the total estimated output requirements will be in terms of annual gross outputs.

See Robert Dorfman, Paul A. Samuelson, and Robert M. Solow, *Linear Programming and Economic Analysis* (New York: McGraw-Hill, 1958) and Hollis Burnley Chenery and Paul Gordon Clark, *Interindustry Economics* (New York: John Wiley and Sons, 1959).

effect on consumption or production decisions. If a second period of activity were analyzed, the adjustments made by producers in the first period would result in additional adjustments in transfer receipts, tax payments, expenditures, production, and earned income. By ignoring these further effects, the model employed in this study assumes full adjustment of consumption and production to program-induced income changes within the period and no second-period or subsequent adjustment of either expenditures or related higher-order effects on production or employment.

The parameters of this module are derived from the Multiregional Input–Output Model (MRIO).[14] MRIO contains 44 regions and 79 industries. Two basic sets of data are intrinsic to it: interindustry transactions within each of the regions, indicating the input structure of all of the industries in a region;[15] and interregional trade flows, indicating the patterns of trade among regions in both final and intermediate outputs.

The version of the MRIO model used in this study contains technical coefficient matrices for 1963,[16] as well as value-added components by industry for that year. Use of this model assumes that industry technologies that existed in 1963 are appropriate for estimating the regional impacts of altered final demands in 1973.

The interregional trade flows contained in MRIO also depict the structure of the economy in 1963. The trade flows between regions contained in the model are developed for 61 industrial sectors[17] and for all of the 44 regions, for products that use the standard modes of transportation and are recorded in the standard transportation statistics. The trade coefficients based on these flows provide a complete specification of interregional commodity shipments among the 44 regions.

In adapting the MRIO model to this study, the 44 regions are col-

---

[14]This model is described in Karen R. Polenske, *The United States Multiregional Input–Output Model* (Lexington, Mass.: Lexington Books, D.C. Heath, forthcoming). It is an adaptation of the multiregional input–output model originally implemented at the Harvard Economic Research Project under a contract with the U.S. Economic Development Administration and other federal government agencies.

[15]The regional technical coefficients in the model represent the total impacts of specific goods or services required by an industry in a region divided by the output of that industry in that region.

[16]U.S. Department of Commerce, Office of Business Economics, "Input–Output Structure of the U.S. Economy: 1963," *Survey of Current Business* 49 (November 1969): 16–47.

[17]Shipments are not estimated for the construction or service industries.

lapsed to the 23 regions defined in Appendix H. This procedure entails the construction of technical coefficient matrices for combined MRIO regions based on weighted averages of MRIO technologies. Interregional trade flows are aggregated to the 23-region level as well.

In constructing the MRIO model, two methods are employed for estimating regional estimates of input–output relationships. It is assumed that agriculture, mining, and construction possess distinctive regional technologies. For example, agriculture is known to rely on highly distinctive production methods even at a subsectoral level of aggregation: Livestock includes range-fed as well as lot-fed herds, and field crops are grown both with and without irrigation. Thus, for the agricultural sectors, techniques of production corresponding to regional conditions are estimated; sector-level technologies are then calculated by weighting appropriate subaggregates. Similar problems arise with respect to mining, in which various production technologies are possible depending on the nature of the deposit, and with respect to construction, in which materials and standards vary substantially by location. In each of these cases, subsector techniques are developed from industry studies and transformed into sector estimates. The totals over all regions are reconciled to the national estimates reported in the 1963 input–output study.[18] Discrepancies between the regional and national estimates are prorated over the regional transactions tables.[19]

In the remaining sectors, regional technical coefficients are assumed to vary only as the mix of products produced by the sector varies. The 370-order national input–output coefficients together with census estimates of outputs for the 370-order classification are then used to calculate an aggregated transactions table. Again, discrepancies between national and regional estimates are prorated over regions.

The interregional trade flows contained in MRIO were obtained from a study conducted by Jack Faucett Associates,[20] in which only 61 of the 79 primary sectors were observed to engage in interregional trade.[21] These flows were estimated from data sources on the standard public

---

[18] U.S. Department of Commerce, Office of Business Economics, "Input–Output Structure, 1963."

[19] The details of the estimation procedures and the data sources are reported in Karen R. Polenske et al., State Estimates of Technology, 1963 (Lexington, Mass.: Lexington Books, D.C. Heath, 1974).

[20] John M. Rodgers, State Estimates of Interregional Commodity Trade, 1963 (Lexington, Mass.: Lexington Books, D.C. Heath, 1973).

[21] These sectors are designated by an asterisk in Appendix G.

modes of transportation.[22] Trade flows were estimated in both value units and tonnage units. The data were obtained largely from sample surveys and probably contain considerable sampling error—perhaps on the order of plus or minus 30 percent.[23]

In this module, then, estimates are made of the implications for gross output of the policy-induced final consumption demands for 79 industries in 23 regions. For each vector of final consumption demand, gross outputs, reflecting both direct and indirect demands, are estimated for the same 79 industries and 23 regions—a total of 1817 estimates of sectoral output for each combined tax–transfer program simulated.

The factor employment module

The fourth module explores the effects of the tax–transfer program on demands for primary factors, particularly labor. The module relies on fixed-coefficients production functions in identifying the derived demands for labor. In the computational version of the module, gross output changes are multiplied by a matrix of coefficients of detailed factor-input requirements to yield estimates of the derived demands for labor by production sector, occupation, and region.

For the occupational analyses, 114 detailed categories are employed in the study. These analyses suggest which occupations are net losers or net gainers because of the policy change or, if all occupations gain, which are relatively small and which are relatively large gainers. From the regional and sectoral estimates of output, evidence is obtained on the policy-induced gains or losses in total employment in 23 regions and 79 production sectors.

---

[22]The data sources included the following: U.S. Department of the Army, Corps of Engineers, *Waterborne Commerce of the United States: Calendar Year 1963*, Compiled under the Supervision of the Resident Member, Board of Engineers for Rivers and Harbors (Washington, D.C.: U.S. Government Printing Office, 1964) (D103.1/2:); U.S. Bureau of the Census, *Census of Transportation, 1963*, vol. 3, *Commodity Transportation Survey* (Washington, D.C.: U.S. Government Printing Office, 1966) (C3.233/3:963/v.3); U.S. Interstate Commerce Commission, Bureau of Economics, *Carload Waybill Statistics, 1963: State-to-State Distribution, All Commodities, Traffic and Revenue, 1 Percent Sample of Terminations in 1963*, Statement SS-1, 1963 (Washington, D.C.: U.S. Government Printing Office, 1966) (IC1.23/11:963); U.S. Department of Agriculture, Marketing Economics Division, Economics Research Service, *For-Hire Motor Carriers Hauling Exempt Agricultural Commodities, Nature and Extent of Operations*, Marketing Research Report no. 585, by Mildred R. DeWolfe (Washington, D.C.: U.S. Government Printing Office, 1963) (A1.82:585); and an unpublished special tabulation of the 1963 Census of Transportation.
[23]Rodgers, *Interregional Commodity Trade*.

Estimation of these effects on employment by occupation is a two-step process. First, the total changes in employment by region and sector are determined by multiplying coefficients of employment per unit of output by the change in gross output for each region and production sector. These employment–output coefficients are derived from Bureau of Labor Statistics estimates of output per man-year for 1947, 1958, and 1963, and from estimates of employment by sector and region reported in the MRIO project.[24] Annual compound rates of productivity growth for each sector are computed for the 1947–1963 period and then employed in aging the 1963 coefficients to 1973.[25] The changes in 1973 employment that would result from the policy-induced gross output changes are then estimated by multiplying the derived 1973 sectoral employment–output coefficients by incremental gross output by production sector.[26]

In the second step of the analysis, the total incremental employment estimates are distributed over 114 occupational categories by multiplying a matrix of the percentage distributions of employment by occupation and industry by the sectoral employment estimates.[27] This matrix of 79 by 114 elements was obtained from a Bureau of Labor Statistics study based on the 1970 U.S. Census.[28] Again it is assumed that, for any sector, patterns of employment in all regions are identical to national patterns. Thus, the procedure implies that all occupations participate in incre-

[24] The MRIO estimates of employment by sector by region were developed from Census Bureau, Bureau of Labor Statistics, and Social Security Administration statistics. See John M. Rodgers, *State Estimates of Outputs, Employment, and Payrolls, 1947, 1958, 1963* (Lexington, Mass.: Lexington Books, D.C. Heath, 1972).

[25] This projection procedure leads to some anomalous estimates for a few of the smaller industries. Where 1973 employment–output ratio projections are unreasonably higher than expected, adjustments are made to produce estimates that conform with the general notion that 40 percent of total output is value added at the average wage. The adjustment procedure is to impose zero productivity growth rates wherever positive estimates of these rates appear—usually as a result of errors in reporting or in measurement of employment or output.

[26] As has been noted, the assumption that average and marginal labor requirements are equal fails to consider that while production workers may be employed in approximate proportion to output in the short run, supervisory and overhead employment will change only modestly in response to output changes. Thus, estimates of total employment effects and, especially, of employment effects for marginal and supervisory occupations are likely to be biased upward.

[27] The description of the 114 occupational categories is presented in Appendix I.

[28] The methodology and the data employed in this study are described in U.S. Department of Labor, Bureau of Labor Statistics, *Tomorrow's Manpower Needs*, bulletin no. 1606, vol. 4, "The National Industry–Occupational Matrix and Other Manpower Data" (Washington, D.C.: U.S. Government Printing Office, 1969) (L2.3:1606/v.4).

mental employment within a sector as they participated in average employment in 1970. From this procedure, estimates of the induced employment in each of 114 occupations in each of 23 regions are obtained.

The income distribution module

The final module evaluates the impact of program-stimulated changes in production and employment on the size distribution of incremental household incomes from salaries and wages. The changes in regional and occupational labor demands are transformed first into changes in employment by earnings class for each of the 23 regions, and then into changes in the size distribution of household income.

In order to project the distribution of incremental earnings by family income class, it is necessary first to estimate the size distribution of incremental earnings by individual earnings class, then to map changes in the distribution of workers' earned income into changes in the distribution of disposable family income. Implementing this procedure requires first determining the relative frequency distribution of all employed members of the labor force by earnings class for each of the 114 occupations and 23 regions—a total of 2622 relative frequency distributions.[29] These distributions are obtained in 15-class detail through a special tabulation from the 1-in-100 sample tapes of the 1970 U.S. Census.[30]

The impact of incremental incomes on the size distribution of household income is simulated under the assumption that new earnings will be distributed on a per capita basis to currently employed workers. The increments are thus assumed to accrue to households with members employed in the affected occupations. The module first determines the increment to earnings that might be expected to result from increases or decreases in employment. In estimating these earnings increments it is assumed that the distribution of income receipts among workers occupying the incremental jobs will be the same as the distribution of

---

[29] Appendix J discusses the procedures for obtaining these distributions and presents a regional summary of them.

[30] In this tabulation, the following 15 earnings classes are employed: less than −$2500; −$2500–$0; $1–$1000; $1000–$2000; $2000–$3000; $3000–$4000; $4000–$5000; $5000–$6000; $6000–$7000; $7000–$8000; $8000–$9000; $9000–$10,000; $10,000–$15,000; $15,000–$20,000; and $20,000 or more.

earnings within the occupation. This in turn implies that the income accruing to the holder of each new job will be the mean income for workers in the occupation in 1970.

Next, the total incremental earnings are distributed to the 15 income classes by size of incremental income. Thus for occupations with a large variance in earnings, several income classes benefit from increased employment. The total increment to earnings in an income class is distributed equally among earners in the class in each region.[31] Finally, these incremental earnings by earner are aggregated into household income classes by assembling individual earners (with their earnings increments) into the household units to which they belong. The aggregation of individual earners (by earnings class) into households (by income class) is accomplished by mapping average earnings increments by earnings class onto individual earners on the CPS tape, identified by earnings, and then aggregating these earners back into their household units.

Aggregating these household income distributions within a region (or the nation) yields the distribution of induced earnings by household income class for the region (or the nation). The structure of these marginal distributions can be compared with the pre-existing income distribution in the region (or the nation) to determine the effect of the policy change in raising or lowering the regional (or national) income distribution or in making it more or less unequal. Similarly, these marginal distributions can be compared to the primary distribution of transfers to determine the extent to which the induced effects of the policy change complement or offset its primary effects.

The model in notational form

In this section, the empirical model described in the previous section is presented in notational form. Uppercase Greek letters represent matrices, and lowercase Latin letters represent column vectors.

---

[31] An infinite number of assumptions could be made regarding the distribution among individuals of the induced jobs and earnings. Labor markets adjust to increments in demand by some combination of employing additional people who have been either unemployed or not in the labor force, moving some employed workers from part-time or part-year work to full-time or full-year work, and inducing overtime work from full-time, full-year workers. Each possible combination would affect the income distribution differently. The combination we have adopted is as arbitrary as any other assumed combination.

The tax–transfer module

The current-income approach. Assume y_s is a vector, each element of which is the 1973 income level of a household included in the 1971 Current Population Survey (CPS). Each household is indexed by family size, place of residence, marital status, and all other sociodemographic characteristics that enter the eligibility and benefit rules of the tax–transfer program to be simulated. Assume Φ is a matrix portraying the eligibility rules and benefit schedules of the program in the form of taxation and/or benefit rates corresponding to each element of y_s. Φ is a diagonal matrix, where Φ_{ii} (the ith element along the diagonal) is the taxation (and/or benefit) rate corresponding to the ith element of y_s. Premultiplying y_s by Φ yields an estimate of the program-induced change in income for each family in the sample population. Call this vector t_s.

$$t_s = \Phi \cdot y_s. \tag{1}$$

Let Ω be a diagonal matrix of weights, which, when applied to t_s, yield national estimates of program-induced income changes.

$$t_n = \Omega \cdot t_s. \tag{2}$$

The summation of all the elements of t_s yields the total national transfer cost (or tax yield) of the program, t_n°. For the combined transfer and taxation programs analyzed in this study, $t_n^{\circ} = 0$ by assumption.

The normal-income approach. This approach accepts the estimates in t_s as the basis for estimating the policy-induced change in *normal* income. The elements of t_s are partitioned into 177 subvectors, t_s^i, on the basis of their demographic characteristics. For the simulation of combined transfer and taxation programs, the mean *net* transfer $\bar{t}_s^i$ received by the members of a group is assigned to each member of the group and a new vector, t_s^*, is formed. The ith element of t_s^* is the expected net transfer received by the ith household in the CPS on the basis of its normal income, which is proxied by the household's permanent characteristics. Let Y be a diagonal matrix, in which $Y_{ii} = t^i/t_s^i$, that is, the ith element along the diagonal is the ratio of the estimates of the ith household's induced change in normal income to its induced change in current income. Then,

$$t_s^* = Y \cdot t_s. \tag{3}$$

Again, we can apply Ω to obtain national estimates of program-induced income changes:

$$t_n{}^* = \Omega \cdot t_s{}^*. \tag{4}$$

A similar calculation can be done for each transfer or taxation program separately, in which case $t_n{}^*$ is a weighted vector of the expected change in normal income for the households represented by the vector elements. Again, $t_n{}^{o*}$ is the total national transfer cost or tax yield, which equals zero in the combined programs analyzed in this study.

The consumption expenditure module

Method 1. Let **M** be a diagonal matrix in which the ith element along the diagonal is the estimated marginal propensity to consume from current income for the ith household. The elements of **M** can assume any of six values depending on the pretransfer income class to which the household belongs. By premultiplying t_n from the transfer module by **M**, we derive a vector, **c**, specifying for each household the weighted total consumption expenditures induced by the tax–transfer program.

$$c = M \cdot t_n. \tag{5}$$

Summing the elements of **c** yields c^o, an estimate of total national personal consumption expenditures induced by the program. For the program analyzed here, $c^o > 0$.

Allocation among commodity categories of the estimated changes in aggregate household expenditures by region is accomplished by multiplying the estimated change in total expenditures for each of the income groups in any region by a vector of estimated marginal budget shares for that income group for the 79 commodity categories. As a first step, **c** can be aggregated into a new vector, **ĉ**, of total expenditures by region and income class. This is possible because the elements of **c** are indexed by region and income. The aggregation is accomplished through an appropriately defined operator matrix, Σ.

$$\hat{c} = \Sigma \cdot c. \tag{6}$$

The estimated marginal budget shares are used to construct a block diagonal matrix, **B**. Each block along the diagonal is a submatrix of marginal budget shares for a region. The ith row of a submatrix is the vector of budget shares for the ith income class for that region. By premultiplying $\hat{\mathbf{c}}$ by $\mathbf{B}$, we obtain $\mathbf{e}$, the vector of commodity-specific expenditures in each region.

$$\mathbf{e} = \mathbf{B} \cdot \hat{\mathbf{c}} \qquad (7)$$

where

$$\mathbf{B} = \begin{pmatrix} \mathbf{B}_1 & & & & \\ & \mathbf{B}_2 & & & \\ & & \mathbf{B}_3 & & \\ & & & \ddots & \\ & & & & \\ & & & & \mathbf{B}_{23} \end{pmatrix}$$

$$\mathbf{B}_i = \begin{pmatrix} \beta_1{}^a & \beta_1{}^b & \cdots & \beta_1{}^n \\ \beta_2{}^a & & & \\ \vdots & & & \\ \vdots & & & \\ \vdots & & & \\ \beta_6{}^a & \cdots & \cdots & \beta_6{}^n \end{pmatrix} \qquad \beta_g{}^h = \frac{MPE_g{}^h}{\sum\limits_{i=a}^{n} MPE_g{}^i} \qquad (8)$$

and in which $MPE_g{}^h$ = the marginal propensity of households in income class g to spend on commodity h. It is assumed that $\mathbf{B}_1 = \mathbf{B}_2 = \cdots = \mathbf{B}_{23}$.

The vector $\mathbf{e}$ has 1817 elements, which are partitioned into 23 subvectors, each giving the commodity-specific estimates of expenditures for a region. By convention, the first 79 elements of $\mathbf{e}$ are the commodity expenditures in the first region, and so on.

Method 2. This approach deals directly with the household unit and develops a measure of normal family income through which the effects of the tax–transfer program operate.

In empirically implementing this approach, the mean income of a socioeconomic group $[\bar{y}_j, j = 1,2,\ldots,177]$ is assigned to each household in the group as the best estimate of its normal income, $y_j{}^p$.

$$y_j{}^p = \bar{y}_j. \qquad (9)$$

By matching groups from the CPS with equivalent groups from the CES, the expected mean expenditures for any socioeconomic group, $\bar{e}_j$, are obtained and assigned to each family in that group, $e_j{}^p$.

$$e_j{}^p = \bar{e}_j. \qquad (10)$$

The ratio e_j^p/y_j^p is taken to be the marginal propensity to spend out of normal income for a household having the socioeconomic characteristics shared by the jth group. A diagonal matrix $\mathbf{M}^*$, analogous to the matrix $\mathbf{M}$ of Method 1, is formed, with the marginal propensities to spend set along the diagonal such that the ith element along the diagonal corresponds to the ith household in the CPS.

The expected net transfers from the normal-income approach of the module, $\mathbf{t}_n^*$, are premultiplied by $\mathbf{M}^*$, yielding a vector, $\mathbf{c}^*$, specifying for each household the expected policy-induced change in total expenditures.

$$\mathbf{c}^* = \mathbf{M}^* \cdot \mathbf{t}_n^*. \tag{11}$$

In the second step of the analysis, a household's change in expenditures is allocated among commodity categories in proportion to the preprogram mean allocation among commodity categories of total expenditures of the household's socioeconomic group. The vector $\mathbf{c}^*$ is then aggregated into a new vector of total expenditures by region and group, $\hat{\mathbf{c}}^*$, by applying an appropriately defined operator matrix, Σ^*.

$$\hat{\mathbf{c}} = \Sigma^* \cdot \mathbf{c}^*. \tag{12}$$

Then a block diagonal matrix of budget shares, $\mathbf{B}^*$, is formed similarly to the matrix $\mathbf{B}$ in Method 1. The only difference is that each $\mathbf{B}_1^*$ is dimensioned 177×79. Again, it is assumed that $\mathbf{B}_1^* = \mathbf{B}_2^* = \ldots = \mathbf{B}_{23}^*$. Premultiplying $\hat{\mathbf{c}}^*$ by $\mathbf{B}^*$ yields $\mathbf{e}^*$, the vector of commodity-specific expenditures of each region.

$$\mathbf{e}^* = \mathbf{B}^* \cdot \hat{\mathbf{c}}^* \tag{13}$$

where

$$\mathbf{B}^* = \begin{pmatrix} \mathbf{B}_1^* & & & \\ & \mathbf{B}_2^* & & \\ & & \ddots & \\ & & & \mathbf{B}_{23}^* \end{pmatrix} \qquad \mathbf{B}_j^* = \begin{pmatrix} \beta_1^a & \beta_1^b & \ldots & \beta_1^n \\ \vdots & & & \\ \beta_{177}^a & & \ldots & \beta_{177}^n \end{pmatrix}$$

$$\beta_g^h = \frac{\overline{e}_g^h}{\overline{e}_g}. \tag{14}$$

Method 3. This method estimates changes in total household expenditures by applying the marginal propensity to spend corresponding to the household's normal income to the program-induced change in normal income. Similarly, the estimated program-induced change in expenditures is allocated among commodities by applying the vector of marginal budget shares corresponding to the household's normal income. While the marginal propensities to spend and the marginal budget shares are estimated from models in which current income is the independent variable, they are considered appropriate in estimating changes in commodity expenditures in response to a change in normal income.

Empirically, this approach is simulated exactly as Method 1 is, except that the transfers used as input are $\mathbf{t}_n^*$. The marginal propensities to spend and marginal budget shares of Method 1 are substituted for those of Method 2 in estimating the change, by region, in the level and item composition of expenditures. For notational convenience, we superscript the resulting vectors with a double asterisk.

$$\mathbf{c}^{**} = \mathbf{M} \cdot \mathbf{t}_n^*. \tag{15}$$

$$\hat{\mathbf{c}}^{**} = \Sigma \cdot \mathbf{c}^{**}. \tag{16}$$

$$\mathbf{e}^{**} = \mathbf{B} \cdot \mathbf{c}^{**}. \tag{17}$$

The gross output module

In the previous module, policy-induced consumption demands were estimated for each of 79 production sectors in each of 23 regions and summarized in an 1817-element vector, $\mathbf{e}(\mathbf{e}^*, \mathbf{e}^{**})$. Let Γ be a square matrix of dimension 1817×1817 made up of 79×79 diagonal matrices. Each element, Γ_i^{gh}, describes the fraction of total consumption of commodity i in region h that is imported from region g. Further define $\hat{\mathbf{A}}$ to be a block diagonal matrix (1817×1817) with 23 square matrices (79×79) of input coefficients along the diagonal describing the structure of production in each region.

$$
\begin{array}{l}
\hat{\mathbf{A}} \\
1817 \times 1817 =
\end{array}
\begin{pmatrix}
\mathbf{A}^1 & & & \\
& \mathbf{A}^2 & & \\
& & \ddots & \\
& & & \mathbf{A}^{23}
\end{pmatrix}
\qquad
\begin{array}{l}
\mathbf{A}^r \\
79 \times 79 =
\end{array}
\begin{pmatrix}
\alpha_{1,1}^r & \cdots & \alpha_{1,79}^r \\
\vdots & & \\
\vdots & & \\
\alpha_{79,1}^r & \cdots & \alpha_{79,79}^r
\end{pmatrix}
\tag{18}
$$

Multiplying $e(e^*, e^{**})$ by the matrix of trade coefficients, Γ, yields the allocation among the regions of final expenditure demands by industry. The resulting vector is multiplied by the inverse of an identity matrix minus the block diagonal matrix of input–output technical coefficients, which has been premultiplied by Γ. This calculation yields an 1817-element vector of gross output, $x(x^*, x^{**})$.

$$x = (I - \Gamma\hat{A})^{-1}\, \Gamma \cdot e. \qquad (19)$$

Calculations similar to that in (19) are done using e^* and e^{**} and carried through the rest of the model. From them, an estimate is obtained of the change in gross output resulting from the policy change in each of 79 industries in each of 23 regions.

The factor employment module

Following the above notation, program-induced employment requirements by industry and region, n, are obtained by multiplying the 1817-element vector of gross output, $x(x^*, x^{**})$, by the matrix of employment–output coefficients, Λ, which is composed of 23 block diagonal 79×79 matrices.

$$n = \Lambda \cdot x. \qquad (20)$$

The occupational composition of the employment requirements is obtained by multiplying the vector of incremental employment by sector and region, $n(n^*, n^{**})$, by the matrix of occupational composition ratios, θ. θ is a block diagonal matrix with submatrices, θ^r, of dimension 114×79, giving the occupational composition ratios by region. In this study, we assumed $\theta^1 = \theta^2 = \cdots = \theta^{23}$. For Method 1 of the expenditure module, the increment to the demand for labor in each of the 114 occupations in each of the 23 regions is given by the vector w. Methods 2 and 3 of the expenditure module yield w^* and w^{**}.

$$w = \theta \cdot n. \qquad (21)$$

The income distribution module

The final step in tracing the effects of the tax–transfer program on the economy is the estimation of the pattern of labor demand, across earnings and income classes, that is generated by the induced changes in consumption expenditures and gross outputs.

The first step of this final module can be stated formally as

$$\mathbf{j} = \Psi \cdot \mathbf{w}, \tag{22}$$

where Ψ is a block diagonal matrix constructed from the 23 regional relative frequency distributions of jobs by earnings class. The submatrices along the diagonal, Ψ^r, are of dimension 15 × 114. The typical element of each submatrix, $\psi_{ij}{}^r$, is the percentage of employees engaged in occupation j belonging to earnings class i. $\mathbf{j}$ is a vector of the distribution of jobs, by regional earnings class, induced by the transfer policy. Again, estimates of $\mathbf{j}^*$ and $\mathbf{j}^{**}$ are obtained for Methods 2 and 3 of the expenditure module.

As a second step, a vector of the earnings increment in each regional earnings class, $\mathbf{b}$, can be obtained by premultiplying $\mathbf{j}$ by a diagonal matrix, π, consisting of the increment to earnings per job in each earnings class in each region. In the simulations of the model, we use the earnings-class average to estimate increased earnings in each regional earnings class.

$$\mathbf{b} = \pi \cdot \mathbf{j}. \tag{23}$$

Finally, the vector of the earnings increment in each regional earnings class, $\mathbf{b}$, is mapped into a vector of the earnings increment in each regional income class, $\mathbf{d}$, by premultiplying $\mathbf{b}$ by a transformation matrix that displays the distribution by income class of earnings by earnings class in a region, $\mathbf{T}$. $\mathbf{T}$ is, again, a block diagonal matrix with square submatrices for each region of dimension 15 × 15 along the diagonal.

$$\mathbf{d} = \mathbf{T} \cdot \mathbf{b}. \tag{24}$$

Each of the 345 elements of $\mathbf{d}$ represents the increment to earnings in one of 15 income classes in one of 23 regions.

5

From first-round to final income redistribution: How much do antipoverty transfers equalize incomes?

The simulation model developed in Chapters 3 and 4 permits a more complete analysis of the distributional impact of alternative income-transfer policies than has heretofore been possible. It permits comparison of a policy's indirect effects on the income distribution with its direct effects and enables us to determine how well the full impact meets the policy's redistributional objectives. As in the case of other prominent legislative actions (on medical care, for example), higher-order economic effects induced by a policy may differ substantially from, or even offset, the direct effects.

In the first section of this chapter, the first-round distributional impacts of the Family Assistance Plan (FAP) and of a negative income tax (NIT) are described and interpreted as revealing the intended distributional effect of the programs. In the second section, the indirect economic impacts stimulated by the same policy measures are discussed. This discussion briefly recounts the analytic steps embodied in the model. The third section presents the indirect distributional consequences of the transfer policies and compares them with the first-round (and presumably intended) effects, in terms of both the pattern of labor demands and the distribution of generated earnings by family income level. In Chapter 6, the empirical results of the intermediate modules—those whose economic processes account for the final distribution effect—are analyzed. These results indicate the nature of the economic adjustments that result in the final distributional impact described here.

First-round distributional effects

The direct net benefits of the tax–transfer scheme are described hereafter as first-round distributional effects. Net benefits are defined as transfer receipts minus tax payments. Thus, program beneficiaries tend to receive positive net benefits, while more affluent taxpayers tend to incur negative net benefits (tax increases). Transfers, taxes, and net benefits under FAP and NIT are analyzed in this section.

In Table 5.1, the total payments of benefits under the two proposals are presented, together with an analysis of the components of FAP (NIT does not entail any modification of existing transfer schemes). Taxes are required to finance the program of payments to beneficiaries. This implies a surtax of 3.57 percent of the federal income tax under FAP and 3.67 percent under NIT.

In Table 5.2, the distribution of gross transfers[1] from FAP and NIT among households grouped by family income is shown for the year 1973. In addition, the percentage distribution of preprogram income is

TABLE 5.1

Aggregate gross transfers of FAP and NIT

Program		Aggregate gross transfers (in millions of dollars)
Family Assistance Plan (FAP)		$3330.4
Federal benefit payments	$4922.1	
AFDC and AFDC-UP	−3467.2	
State supplementary benefits	1875.5	
Negative income tax (NIT)		$3420.6

[1]For NIT, gross transfers are the negative-tax benefits received; for FAP, gross transfers are the federal negative-tax benefits received, plus state supplementation payments, minus the reduction in benefits from the discontinued AFDC and AFDC-UP programs. For both programs, *net* transfers account for the taxes required to finance the program, and are equivalent to changes in personal disposable income.

TABLE 5.2
Distribution of gross transfers of FAP and NIT, by income class

Income class	FAP					NIT				
	Percentage distribution of preprogram income	Gross transfers (in millions of dollars)	Transfers per recipient family	Transfers per family	Percentage of families receiving transfers	Gross transfers (in millions of dollars)	Percentage distribution of gross transfers	Transfers per recipient family	Transfers per family	Percentage of families receiving transfers
Less than $1000	.04	$1121.9	$2515	$580	23.1	$ 991.9	29.0	$2218	$512	23.1
$1000–$2000	.74	839.7	1691	230	13.6	824.3	24.1	1626	225	13.9
$2000–$3000	1.34	786.3	1110	189	17.1	812.2	23.7	1141	195	17.1
$3000–$4000	1.61	503.1	702	143	20.4	524.3	15.3	708	148	21.0
$4000–$5000	1.92	222.0	445	68	15.3	208.9	6.1	544	64	11.7
$5000–$6000	2.24	85.7	246	27	11.2	56.6	1.7	314	18	5.8
$6000–$10,000	13.98	106.9	21	1	3.9	2.5	.1	123	1	.6
$10,000–$15,000	24.30	−200.9	−1596	−13	.9	—	—	—	—	—
$15,000–$20,000	20.24	−107.2	−1890	−12	.6	—	—	—	—	—
More than $20,000	33.59	−27.2	−1235	−3	.3	—	—	—	—	—
Total	100.0	3330.4	846	50	6.0	3420.7	100.0	1144	52	4.5

55

TABLE 5.3
Distribution of taxes required to finance FAP and NIT, by income class

Income class	Percentage distribution of preprogram income	FAP Percentage distribution of taxes	FAP Taxes (in millions of dollars)	FAP Taxes per family	NIT Taxes (in millions of dollars)	NIT Taxes per family
Less than $1000	.04	.0	$ .1	$ .03	$ .1	$ .03
$1000–$2000	.74	.0	.3	.07	.3	.07
$2000–$3000	1.34	.1	3.6	.86	3.7	.89
$3000–$4000	1.61	.3	9.4	2.66	9.7	2.73
$4000–$5000	1.92	.6	21.4	6.58	22.1	6.77
$5000–$6000	2.24	.9	30.4	9.73	31.2	9.98
$6000–$10,000	13.98	9.2	308.7	23.08	317.5	23.73
$10,000–$15,000	24.30	21.1	701.8	46.69	721.4	47.90
$15,000–$20,000	20.24	20.5	680.9	75.63	699.3	77.57
More than $20,000	33.59	47.3	1573.8	175.39	1615.4	179.89
Total	100.0	100.0	3330.4	50.45	3420.7	51.69

shown. As expected, a large share of the gross benefits from each of the programs goes to households at the bottom end of the income distribution.[2] In both plans, over $2.5 billion is transferred to households with preprogram incomes less than $3000—an average benefit of about $1700 per recipient family. These same families receive only about 2.1 percent of the nation's personal income.

The data on gross benefits per recipient family confirm the substantial antipoverty direct impact of FAP and NIT. For FAP, annual gross transfers are more than $2500 for eligible family units with less than $1000 of other income. NIT awards gross transfers of more than $2200 to such families. In both programs, gross transfers decline steadily with household income. Average benefits per recipient family are $846 for FAP and $1144 for NIT. Of households in the lowest income class, 23.1 percent are covered by both programs, while of households with incomes in the $6000–$10,000 range, only 3.9 percent are covered by FAP and 0.6 percent by NIT.[3] FAP provides gross transfers to 6.0 percent of the household units in the nation; NIT to 4.5 percent.

Table 5.3 presents the first-round distributional effects of the taxes required to finance both FAP and NIT. Given the structure of the U.S. personal income tax, the distributional pattern of the tax simulation is not surprising. Trivial increases in taxes are imposed on families with incomes less than $3000. While families with incomes less than $6000 receive about 8 percent of the nation's personal income, they pay only about 2 percent of the taxes required to finance the transfer proposals. About two-thirds of the required taxes are paid by families with incomes over $15,000. The progressiveness of this distribution of program costs can be observed by comparing the percentage distribution of tax costs with the percentage distribution of preprogram income. Financing the proposals requires increased taxes of approximately $50 per year per household.

---

[2]The percentage calculation for FAP is not shown. Because some income classes show negative gross benefits, calculation of a percentage distribution over the entire income range is impossible. The negative benefits shown for the higher income classes are attributable to the stipulation that no state supplementation benefits be paid to families with preprogram incomes in excess of $10,000. Because some families with incomes in excess of $10,000 were receiving AFDC and AFDC-UP benefits (primarily families caring for children other than their own, for example, foster parents), FAP, with its elimination of AFDC and AFDC-UP benefits, results in negative gross transfers for these households.

[3]These low coverage ratios are attributable to the exclusion from the program of unrelated individuals and couples without children.

The economic impact of tax–transfer policy

TABLE 5.4

Distribution of net transfers of FAP and NIT, by income class

	FAP		NIT	
Income class	Net benefits (in millions of dollars)	Net benefits per family	Net benefits (in millions of dollars)	Net benefits per family
Less than $1000	$1121.8	$628.54	$991.8	$511.69
$1000–$2000	839.4	230.25	824.0	225.08
$2000–$3000	782.7	188.56	808.5	193.74
$3000–$4000	493.7	140.20	514.7	145.58
$4000–$5000	200.6	61.56	186.8	57.13
$5000–$6000	55.3	17.70	25.4	8.12
$6000–$10,000	−201.8	−15.09	−315.0	−23.54
$10,000–$15,000	−902.7	−60.05	−721.4	−47.90
$15,000–$20,000	−788.1	−87.52	−699.3	−77.57
More than $20,000	−1601.0	−178.42	−1615.4	−179.89

Table 5.4 shows the net effects of both the gross transfers and the taxes required to finance them. For FAP and NIT, net transfers accrue to all income classes below $6000; net costs accrue to all income classes above $6000. The extent of the income redistribution accomplished by the plans is indicated by the disparities between the lowest and highest income classes. Under FAP, families with incomes in excess of $15,000 are estimated to lose $2.4 billion, while households with incomes less than $2000 are estimated to gain nearly $2.0 billion. Similarly, for NIT, families with incomes less than $2000 gain about $1.8 billion, while families with incomes greater than $15,000 lose about $2.3 billion. Families with incomes between $4000 and $15,000—the bulk of U.S. households—are relatively unaffected by either of the plans. For both FAP and NIT, the total gain of all income classes in this range showing a net gain (classes from $4000 to $6000) is less than $.3 billion and the total loss of all classes in this range showing a net loss (classes from $6000 to $15,000) is approximately $1.1 billion.

When the gains and losses for FAP are looked at for all families, the average net benefit for families in the lowest income class is more than $625 and the average net loss to families in the highest income class is about $180. For NIT, the average net benefit is smaller—$510 for the lowest income class—while the average family in the highest income class again experiences a net loss of about $180. The average family with about $7000–$8000 of preprogram income experiences no net gain or loss from either plan. These values are averages for all families in the income class, not for beneficiaries or taxpayers only.

This first-round redistribution from higher to lower income classes is reflected in a narrowing of the income distribution. Prior to implementation of either program, the estimated Gini coefficient for the distribution of current family income is .435. Under either FAP or NIT and its surtax financing arrangement, the inequality of the distribution of family income is reduced; the postprogram Gini coefficient is .426, a reduction of nearly .01.[4]

Evidence on the programs' first-round impacts on the size distribution of income is complemented by information on their first-round regional effects. Because low-income families tend to be concentrated spatially—in the South, in northern urban areas, in Appalachia—any program designed to redistribute income from higher to lower income classes will also have disparate regional effects.

The distribution among 23 regions of gross program benefits from FAP and NIT is shown in Table 5.5. For both programs, the southern states are the major beneficiaries, receiving 47 percent of total gross benefits from FAP and 45 percent from NIT. Of the southern states, Mississippi is the primary beneficiary, receiving $225 million in FAP transfers (6.8 percent of the total) and $187 million in NIT transfers (5.5 percent of the total).

The Northeast receives about 10 percent of total gross transfers under FAP and about 15 percent under NIT. The North Central region receives nearly 20 percent under FAP and 23 percent under NIT, while the western region receives about 23 percent under FAP and only 17 percent under NIT. The significant disparity between the shares of benefits going to the Northeast under the two programs is attributable to the programs' differential treatment of income from other transfers. Under FAP, for example, AFDC and AFDC-UP are presumed to be terminated—their benefits tend to be reduced by a dollar for every dollar of FAP payments. NIT transfers, on the other hand, decrease by only a percentage of the benefits received from other programs. Hence, in the regions with relatively generous AFDC and AFDC-UP programs (such as the Northeast), gross transfers from FAP will be smaller than those from NIT.

---

[4]The procedure for estimating the Gini coefficient is from N. C. Kakwani and N. Podder, "On the Estimation of Lorenz Curves from Grouped Data," *International Economic Review* 14 (June 1973): 278–292. For both the preprogram and the postprogram distributions, the standard error of the Gini coefficient is .01.

TABLE 5.5

Distribution of gross transfers of FAP and NIT, by region

Region	FAP					NIT			
	Percentage distribution of national income	Total transfers (in millions of dollars)	Percentage distribution of gross transfers	Ratio of percentage of gross transfers to percentage of national income	Per-family transfers	Total transfers (in millions of dollars)	Percentage distribution of gross transfers	Ratio of percentage of gross transfers to percentage of national income	Per-family transfers
Northeast	26.4	$ 342.5	10.3	.39	$ 21.36	$ 504.6	14.7	.56	$ 31.48
(1) Ct, Me, Ma, NH, RI, Vt	6.2	125.1	3.8	.61	32.84	134.5	3.9	.63	35.33
(2) NY	10.5	41.3	1.2	.11	6.94	146.8	4.3	.41	24.70
(3) Pa, NJ	9.7	176.1	5.3	.55	28.05	223.3	6.5	.67	35.57
North Central	28.3	660.1	19.8	.70	35.83	776.9	22.8	.81	42.18
(4) Oh, Mi	9.9	111.0	3.3	.33	17.38	215.9	6.3	.64	33.82
(5) In, Il	8.7	203.7	6.1	.70	37.37	208.0	6.1	.70	38.16
(6) Wi, Mn	3.9	108.9	3.3	.85	37.43	126.0	3.7	.94	43.30
(7) Ia, Mo	3.5	129.5	3.9	1.11	58.37	118.5	3.5	.99	53.39
(8) Ks, Nb, ND, SD	2.3	107.0	3.2	1.39	73.44	108.5	3.2	1.38	74.52

60

	27.4	1554.2	46.7	1.70	79.01	1554.8	45.5	1.66	79.05
South									
(9) De, DC, Md	2.9	53.6	1.6	.55	30.16	83.2	2.4	.84	46.81
(10) Va, WV	2.9	101.5	3.0	1.03	59.18	96.8	2.8	.98	56.44
(11) NC	2.1	127.3	3.8	1.81	81.12	113.9	3.3	1.59	72.37
(12) SC	1.0	91.1	2.7	2.70	106.61	100.0	2.9	2.92	115.51
(13) Ga	2.0	42.3	1.3	.65	28.76	79.4	2.3	1.16	53.42
(14) Fl	3.3	129.1	3.9	1.18	55.76	118.2	3.5	1.05	51.09
(15) Ky, Tn	2.9	163.1	4.9	1.69	74.96	157.0	4.6	1.58	71.79
(16) Al	1.3	112.9	3.4	2.62	112.38	102.6	3.0	2.31	102.09
(17) Ms	0.7	225.2	6.8	9.71	276.53	187.1	5.5	7.82	229.76
(18) Ar, Ok	1.8	83.4	2.5	1.39	66.05	84.1	2.5	1.37	66.60
(19) La	1.4	176.3	5.3	3.79	137.96	164.0	4.8	3.43	128.40
(20) Tx	5.1	248.4	7.5	1.47	72.32	268.5	7.9	1.54	76.01
West	18.2	773.9	23.2	1.27	64.93	584.1	17.1	.94	49.00
(21) Az, Co, Id, NM, Ut, Nv, Wy, Mt, Ak	4.1	194.7	5.8	1.41	72.44	206.1	6.0	1.47	76.68
(22) Wa, Or, Hi	3.1	90.9	2.7	.87	42.66	118.0	3.5	1.11	55.40
(23) Ca	11.0	488.3	14.7	1.34	68.76	260.0	7.6	.69	36.62
United States	100.0	3330.4	100.0		50.43	3420.6	100.0		51.69

61

Of the detailed regions, California gains most in the FAP simulation—receiving 14.7 percent of gross FAP transfers. Texas obtains the largest share of NIT gross transfers—$268 million or 7.9 percent of the total. New York is the smallest recipient under FAP. This is again attributable to the assumed termination of the AFDC and AFDC-UP programs.

These same patterns are also shown in the columns displaying per-family transfers and the regional preference ratio (the ratio of the percentage of gross transfers received by a region to its percentage of national income). In terms of per-family transfers, the South is a substantially larger recipient of both FAP and NIT gross transfers than the other regions; per-family gross transfers to the South are $79, while the next-highest per-family gross transfers are $65 for FAP and $49 for NIT, both accruing to the West. Similarly, while the preference ratio is 1.7 for the South—indicating that its percentage of gross transfers is 1.7 times its percentage of national income—the ratios for the other major regions range from .4 to 1.27 for FAP and from .6 to .9 for NIT.

In the FAP simulation, the preference ratio for Mississippi is 9.7 and is reflected in a per-family gross transfer more than five times the national average. New York (.1) and Ohio-Michigan (.3) have the lowest preference ratios; New York also has the lowest per-family gross transfer ($7). This figure is about 15 percent of the national average of per-family gross transfers, $50. Of the 12 regions included in the South, 10 have preference indicators greater than unity; only 4 regions outside the South have indicators greater than unity. Similarly, of the 14 regions with per-family transfers higher than the national average per-family transfer, 10 are in the South.

Under NIT, per-family gross transfers range from $230 in Mississippi to about $25 in New York. The West receives nearly $50 per family, the North Central region $42, and the Northeast only $31.

The pattern of regional liabilities for financing the transfer programs, shown in Table 5.6, contrasts markedly with the pattern of transfers. While the South receives more than 45 percent of the gross transfers from FAP and NIT, it pays only 26 percent of the taxes required to finance the programs. Conversely, while the Northeast receives nearly 10 percent of gross transfers from FAP and 15 percent from NIT, it pays 27 percent of the taxes required to finance these programs. The same pattern holds for the North Central region. The West receives more in gross transfers from FAP, but less from NIT, than it is required to pay in taxes.

For the more detailed regions, the differences are even larger. New York, for example, receives 1 percent of the gross benefits of FAP while paying 11 percent of the tax costs. For nearly all of the southern regions, the dollar value and percentage of gross benefits exceed the dollar value and percentage of tax costs. Mississippi, the lowest-income state, bears less than 1 percent of the tax costs, while receiving nearly 7 percent of gross transfers from FAP and about 5.5 percent of gross transfers from NIT.

Again, the regional preference ratios and per-family estimates summarize this pattern. Of the 11 regions with ratios less than unity, 7 are in the South; of the 15 regions with per-family taxes lower than the national average, 9 are in the South.

The net effect of these regional gains and costs is shown in Table 5.7. On balance, the South is a substantial net gainer under both of the simulated plans—approximately $680 million for FAP and $655 million for NIT. Of the other three major regions, each experiences net costs under NIT and only the West experiences a small net gain ($140 million) under FAP.

For both plans, the largest *net* gainers are the regions of Mississippi ($204 million from FAP and $165 million from NIT) and Louisiana ($136 million from FAP and $123 million from NIT); the largest net losers are New York and Ohio–Michigan from FAP (−$318 million and −$241 million) and New York and California from NIT (−$222 million and −$157 million). Clearly, gains and losses vary more among the regions under FAP than under NIT, even though the two programs are approximately the same size. The larger variance under FAP is caused by the total loss of AFDC and AFDC-UP benefits and the impact of state supplementation benefits.

Describing the pattern of net transfers either in per-family terms or in terms of the regional impact indicator[5] makes these regional comparisons even more clear. Under FAP, for example, the average New York family stands to lose $54, the average California family stands to gain $12, and the average Mississippi family stands to gain $251. While the average families in the South and the West stand to gain from FAP

---

[5]The regional impact indicator is dollars of *net* transfers to a region divided by .001 times the total income in the region (in 1973 dollars). Symbolically,

$$I_r^{\,n} = \frac{N_r}{.001(Y_r)}$$

where $I_r^{\,n}$ is the regional impact indicator for region r, N_r is the net transfers accruing to region r because of the program, and Y_r is the aggregate income in region r (expressed in 1973 dollars).

TABLE 5.6
Distribution of taxes required to finance FAP and NIT, by region

Region	FAP and NIT		FAP		NIT	
	Percentage distribution of taxes	Ratio of percentage of taxes to percentage of national income	Total taxes (in millions of dollars)	Per-family taxes	Total taxes (in millions of dollars)	Per-family taxes
Northeast	26.9	1.02	$ 896.9	$55.97	$ 920.3	$57.41
(1) Ct, Me, Ma, NH, RI, Vt	5.7	.92	190.6	50.07	195.6	51.36
(2) NY	10.8	1.03	359.6	60.51	369.0	62.07
(3) Pa, NJ	10.4	1.07	346.7	55.24	355.7	56.67
North Central	27.8	.98	925.7	50.28	950.1	51.58
(4) Oh, Mi	10.6	1.07	352.1	55.15	361.2	56.57
(5) In, Il	8.7	1.00	289.2	53.08	296.8	54.45
(6) Wi, Mn	4.0	1.03	134.0	46.08	137.6	47.28
(7) Ia, Mo	2.7	.77	90.1	40.61	92.4	41.66
(8) Ks, Nb, ND, SD	1.8	.78	60.3	41.53	62.1	42.61

South	26.2	.96	873.9	44.46	899.8	45.75
(9) De, DC, Md	3.5	1.21	115.2	64.84	118.1	66.48
(10) Va, WV	2.6	.90	87.2	50.95	89.6	52.25
(11) NC	1.8	.86	59.7	38.05	61.6	39.11
(12) SC	1.0	1.00	32.4	38.05	33.5	38.73
(13) Ga	1.8	.90	61.6	41.92	63.5	42.72
(14) Fl	3.6	1.09	119.5	51.67	122.7	53.01
(15) Ky, Tn	2.4	.83	79.0	36.31	81.6	37.33
(16) Al	1.3	1.00	43.2	43.00	44.3	44.11
(17) Ms	0.6	.86	21.1	25.91	21.6	26.58
(18) Ar, Ok	1.4	.78	46.0	36.44	47.2	37.41
(19) La	1.2	.86	40.1	31.46	41.2	32.26
(20) Tx	5.1	1.00	169.0	49.20	174.9	49.50
West	19.0	1.04	633.8	53.20	650.3	54.56
(21) Az, Co, Id, NM, Ut, Nv, Wy, Mt, Ak	3.8	.93	125.3	46.65	128.6	47.86
(22) Wa, Or, Hi	3.1	1.00	102.4	48.11	105.1	49.34
(23) Ca	12.2	1.11	406.1	57.21	416.6	58.68
United States			3330.4	50.45	3420.6	51.69

65

TABLE 5.7
Distribution of net transfers of FAP and NIT, by region

Region	FAP			NIT		
	Total net transfers (in millions of dollars)	Impact indicator	Per-family net transfers	Total net transfers (in millions of dollars)	Impact indicator	Per-family net transfers
Northeast	$-554.4	-2.25	$-34.60	$-415.5	-1.69	$-25.92
(1) Ct, Me, Ma, NH, RI, Vt	-65.5	-1.14	-17.23	-61.0	-1.05	-16.03
(2) NY	-318.3	-3.26	-53.57	-222.1	-2.27	-37.37
(3) Pa, NJ	-170.6	-1.88	-27.19	-132.4	-1.46	-21.10
North Central	-265.6	-1.01	-14.44	-173.1	-.66	-9.40
(4) Oh, Mi	-241.1	-2.61	-37.76	-145.2	-1.58	-22.75
(5) In, Il	-85.5	-1.06	-15.70	-88.8	-1.10	-16.28
(6) Wi, Mn	-25.1	-.70	-8.66	-11.6	-.32	-3.98
(7) Ia, Mo	39.4	1.21	17.76	26.0	.77	11.73
(8) Ks, Nb, ND, SD	46.7	2.12	31.92	46.5	2.11	31.91

	680.1	2.68	34.56	655.0	2.58	33.30
South						
(9) De, DC, Md	−61.6	−2.24	−34.67	−35.0	−1.27	−19.68
(10) Va, WV	14.3	.53	8.22	7.2	.27	4.19
(11) NC	67.6	3.48	43.09	52.4	2.69	33.26
(12) SC	58.7	6.37	68.60	66.5	7.23	76.79
(13) Ga	−19.3	−1.06	−13.13	15.9	.88	10.70
(14) Fl	9.6	.31	4.10	−4.5	−.15	−1.92
(15) Ky, Tn	84.1	3.16	38.66	75.4	2.83	34.46
(16) Al	69.7	5.96	69.38	58.2	4.98	57.97
(17) Ms	204.1	29.58	250.60	165.5	23.98	203.19
(18) Ar, Ok	37.4	2.25	29.63	36.9	2.22	29.20
(19) La	136.1	10.39	106.53	122.8	9.38	96.14
(20) Tx	79.4	1.69	23.11	93.7	1.99	26.51
West	140.0	.82	11.73	−66.2	−.39	−5.55
(21) Az, Co, Id, NM, Ut, Nv, Wy, Mt, Ak	69.4	1.80	25.78	77.5	2.01	28.82
(22) Wa, Or, Hi	−11.6	−.40	−5.44	12.9	.44	6.06
(23) Ca	82.2	.80	11.56	−156.6	1.52	−22.05

($35 and $12, respectively), the average families in the Northeast and North Central regions stand to lose ($35 and $14, respectively). While the numbers are different, the same relative pattern holds for the per-family net transfers under NIT, except that the average western family switches from being a small net gainer under FAP to being a small net loser under NIT.

Induced distributional effects

The effects of income transfers and corresponding taxes are modified by the economy through induced effects on expenditure, production, and employment. The structure of this process is spelled out in Chapters 3 and 4. Because transfer policy is explicitly concerned with affecting households with certain attributes, a detailed analysis of the induced effects is of interest. In this section, the ultimate indirect impact of the transfer programs on the distribution of income is compared with the distribution of net program benefits. First, the pattern of induced labor demands for high-wage, high-skill workers relative to that for low-wage, low-skill workers is depicted. The annual earnings level of workers serves as a proxy for position on the continuum from low-wage, low-skill to high-wage, high-skill employment. Second, these implicit earnings distributions are mapped into household income distributions to depict the effect of the induced demands on the equality of the size distribution of income. In this final comparison, the distribution of program-generated earned income can be compared to the preprogram income distribution and to the income distribution after direct net transfers.

In evaluating the pattern of program-induced labor demand for workers of various skill levels, it is assumed that the earnings distribution of incremental jobs in a detailed occupation and region is equal to the earnings distribution of all workers in that occupation and region. From these detailed occupational estimates, the distribution of earnings from the induced labor demands can be obtained for any region by aggregating occupations within the region. If the induced labor demands are concentrated at the bottom end of the earnings distribution (relative to the existing distribution of labor), the program can be said to have stimulated the demand for low-skill, low-wage labor. Conversely, if the induced labor demands are concentrated among high earnings classes (relative to the existing pattern of labor demand), the policy change can be said to have stimulated the demand for high-skill, high-wage labor. In the first case, employment opportunities for workers of low-wage, low-skill classes expand to a relatively greater extent than those for workers of other skill levels, and the program's indirect impact can be said to complement its first-round distributional impact. In the second case, high-skill, high-wage classes are relative beneficiaries, and the indirect effects tend to offset the intended or first-round distributional impact.

Both FAP and NIT result in an increase in aggregate labor demand for nearly all regions and for the nation. This increase is due to the lower marginal propensity to consume of higher-income groups (who are net cost bearers and, hence, reduce their expenditures) relative to lower-income groups (who are net beneficiaries and, hence, increase their expenditures). For FAP, the aggregate increase in labor demand is estimated to be about 125,000 jobs; for NIT, the increase is estimated to be about 120,000 jobs. As a result, the high-wage–low-wage comparisons to be described focus on *relative* labor demand impacts among the earnings classes. The benchmark used is the composition of labor demands by earnings class prior to the program. For each earnings class in each region, the question is asked: "Is the share of induced labor demand for the class greater than or less than the share of total labor demand for the class that existed prior to the program?" If the induced share is greater than the pre-existing share, the program shifts the composition of employment toward that earnings class; if the induced share is less than the pre-existing share, the program shifts employment toward other earnings classes.

The program's effect on any skill or earnings class is measured by an impact indicator,[6] which compares the induced labor demand in a regional earnings class with the pre-existing employment in that class. Hence, the indicators are comparable across earnings classes in a region and within an earnings class across regions. Within a region, the earnings-class impact indicators vary around the regional impact indicator. Earnings classes with impact indicators greater than that of the region as a whole experience relative increases in labor demand and employment

---

[6]The earnings-class impact indicator is the ratio of induced labor demand in a regional earnings class to 1970 employment in that earnings class times .001. Symbolically,

$$I_r{}^s = \frac{M_r}{.001\,(P_r)}$$

where $I_r{}^s$ is the impact indicator for an earnings class, M_r is the program-induced change in employment in that earnings class, and P_r is the total 1970 employment in that earnings class.

within the region; those with indicators smaller than the regional indicator experience reductions in their shares of regional employment. Similar comparative statements can be made for a regional earnings class relative to the national impact indicator.

In Tables 5.8 and 5.9, the effects of FAP and NIT on the demand for workers of various skill levels are presented for 23 detailed regions, 4 census regions, and the entire United States.[7] In the full simulation, 15 earnings classes are distinguished and the separate impacts of gross transfers, taxes, and net transfers are estimated. In the tables, the 15 income classes are collapsed into 4 and only the results of the *net* transfers are shown.

Table 5.8 presents earnings-class impact indicators for 23 detailed regions, 4 census regions, and the nation for the *net transfers* from FAP, along with the regional impact indicators and the aggregate man-years of induced employment.

One pattern dominates in Table 5.8.[8] For 19 of the 23 detailed regions, the lowest earnings class (with less than $4000 of annual earnings) has the lowest impact indicator, and consequently a lower indicator than the region as a whole. In 3 of the remaining 4 detailed regions, the impact indicator of the lowest earnings class lies below that of the region, even though it is not the lowest among the earnings-class impact indicators.

The opposite result is observed for the higher earnings classes. The $10,000–$20,000 earnings class has the highest impact indicator in 9 of the 23 regions, and in *no* region is the impact indicator for this earnings class below that for the region as a whole.

The results for the highest earnings class (more than $20,000), show a similar pattern: For 13 of the 23 regions, the impact indicator for this earnings class exceeds that for any other earnings class. Somewhat unexpectedly, the indicator for this class is the lowest in 5 of the 23 regions.

---

[7]This analysis is based on Simulations I and II—the models for FAP and NIT based on current income and marginal budget shares. The estimates for the variants of NIT based on normal income (Simulations III and IV) are not shown. In these normal-income models, the aggregate employment impacts from net transfers are relatively small— 12,000 jobs in Simulation III and 53,000 in Simulation IV. The distributional pattern of Simulation IV is very close to that of Simulation II. In addition to inducing minimal labor demands, Simulation III forecasts a distribution of demands that slightly favors low-wage, low-skill workers relative to high-wage, high-skill workers.

[8]In each region, the highest and lowest impact indicators are noted in the tables. The lowest indicator in a region is marked with an asterisk (*); the highest indicator in a region is marked with a dagger (†).

However, if the two highest earnings classes are collapsed, the lowest earnings class has the lowest impact indicator and the highest class has the highest indicator in all of the regions, with the sole exception of New York.

This same pattern of effects of FAP is present when the detailed regions are collapsed into the four census regions. In three of the four census regions, the lowest earnings class has the lowest impact indicator. Conversely, in all but one of the census regions, one of the two highest earnings classes has the highest impact indicator. For the nation as a whole, the lowest impact indicator is that for the $4000–$10,000 earnings class and the highest impact indicator is that for the more-than-$20,000 earnings class. While the national distribution of induced employment does tend to favor higher-skill relative to lower-skill classes, the difference is relatively small. The lowest impact indicator for a class is 98 percent of the impact indicator for the nation as a whole. The highest impact indicator for a class is 106 percent of that for the nation.

In Table 5.9, the impact indicators for NIT are shown. The relatively adverse employment effect on low-skill workers is somewhat more pronounced for this program than for FAP. For 21 of the 23 detailed regions, the smallest impact indicator belongs to the lowest earnings class. Conversely, the highest impact indicator is found in the highest two earnings classes in all of the 23 regions. When these detailed regions are aggregated into census regions, three of the four lowest regional impact indicators are found in the lowest earnings class and all of the highest regional indicators are found in the highest two classes. For the entire United States, the lowest indicator belongs to the $4000–$10,000 class (with the lowest earnings class being a close second), while the highest earnings class receives the largest relative impact. The lowest impact indicator for a class is 97 percent, and the highest indicator for a class is 106 percent, of the indicator for the nation as a whole. Among the detailed regions, the variation in these percentages is much greater. For South Carolina, for example, the lowest indicator is 72 percent, and the highest indicator is 238 percent, of the indicator for the entire South.

The indirect regional redistribution effects can be observed by comparing the regional impact indicators in Tables 5.8 and 5.9 with those in Table 5.7. In general, the pattern observed is as follows: While the southern regions tend to experience more induced employment than the other regions, their advantage is not nearly as pronounced as it seemed from the first-round distributional analysis. For example,

TABLE 5.8

Earnings-class impact indicators for net transfers of FAP, by region

Region	Earnings Class				Regional impact indicator	Induced employment (in thousands of jobs)
	Less than $4000	$4000–$10,000	$10,000–$20,000	More than $20,000		
Northeast	−.15†	−.18	−.16	−.38*	−.17	−4.5
(1) Ct, Ma, Me, NH, RI, Vt	.22*	.28	.39†	.38	.28	1.6
(2) NY	−.71†	−.85	−.85	−1.15*	−.89	−7.3
(3) Pa, NJ	.06*	.17	.25†	.10	.14	1.2
North Central	.80*	.93	1.00†	.97	.88	22.9
(4) Oh, Mi	−.18	.12	.22†	−.29*	.01	.1
(5) In, Il	.68*	.85	1.05†	1.02	.82	6.2
(6) Wi, Mn	.94*	1.11	1.27	1.35†	1.07	4.1
(7) Ia, Mo	1.82*	2.01	2.24	2.53†	1.97	6.7
(8) Ka, Nb, ND, SD	2.37*	2.51	3.00	3.43†	2.53	5.8

72

South	2.69*	2.86	3.47†	3.28	2.83	76.8
(9) De, DC, Md	-.34	-.21	-.11†	-.58*	-.25	-.6
(10) Va, WV	1.29*	1.62	1.74†	1.43	1.44	3.8
(11) NC	2.58*	2.68	4.38	5.18†	2.80	6.6
(12) SC	3.23*	4.45	6.54	10.54†	4.48	4.9
(13) Ga	.41*	.51	.84†	.41*	.49	1.0
(14) Fl	.97*	1.13	1.31	1.43†	1.04	3.0
(15) Ky, Tn	2.93*	3.21	4.80	5.77†	3.28	9.9
(16) Al	3.68*	4.24	5.20†	5.18	4.07	5.7
(17) Ms	15.93	19.83	30.29†	15.35*	18.15	15.5
(18) Ar, Ok	2.23*	2.56	3.29	3.65†	2.48	4.8
(19) La	7.48*	8.43	10.04	12.05†	8.23	11.3
(20) Tx	2.02*	2.28	2.83	2.89†	2.23	10.9
West	1.68*	1.77	1.95	2.44†	1.78	28.3
(21) Az, Co, Id, NM, Ut, Nv, Wy, Mt, Ak	2.08*	2.25	2.45	2.91†	2.22	8.4
(22) Wa, Or, Hi	.78*	.88	1.00	1.14†	.86	2.5
(23) Ca	1.80*	1.87	2.07	2.61†	1.92	17.4
United States	1.37	1.32*	1.41	1.43†	1.35	123.5

TABLE 5.9

Earnings-class impact indicators for net transfers of NIT, by region

Region	Earnings Class				Regional impact indicator	Induced employment (in thousands of jobs)
	Less than $4000	$4000–$10,000	$10,000–$20,000	More than $20,000		
Northeast	.03*	.11	.17†	.05	.08	2.1
(1) Ct, Ma, Me, NH, RI, Vt,	.29*	.36	.46	.48†	.36	2.0
(2) NY	−.29	−.30	−.25†	−.42*	−.32	−2.7
(3) Pa, NJ	.22*	.35	.46†	.39	.32	2.8
North Central	1.00*	1.12	1.23	1.29†	1.08	23.1
(4) Oh, Mi	.45*	.67	.84†	.61	.55	5.8
(5) In, Il	.65*	.83	1.03†	1.00	.80	6.1
(6) Wi, Mn	1.17*	1.34	1.54	1.69†	1.31	5.0
(7) Ia, Mo	1.58*	1.76	1.96	2.21†	1.72	5.9
(8) Ka, Nb, ND, SD	2.34*	2.48	2.95	3.39†	2.50	5.7

South	2.54*	2.72	3.35†	3.22	2.69	72.9
(9) De, DC, Md	.22*	.29	.43†	.23	.28	.7
(10) Va, WV	1.12*	1.44	1.54†	1.27	1.27	3.3
(11) NC	2.30*	2.39	3.87	4.32†	2.49	5.8
(12) SC	3.58*	4.93	7.25	11.82†	4.97	5.5
(13) Ga	1.10*	1.22	1.89	1.72†	1.24	2.5
(14) Fl	.78*	.92	1.08	1.15†	.84	2.4
(15) Ky, Tn	2.51*	2.72	4.26	4.76†	2.81	8.4
(16) Al	3.28*	3.85	4.67	4.76†	3.66	5.1
(17) Ms	13.16	16.40	25.08†	12.56*	15.00	12.8
(18) Ar, Ok	2.07*	2.34	3.11†	3.05	2.29	4.4
(19) La	6.76*	7.66	9.19	10.88†	7.47	10.2
(20) Tx	2.15*	2.43	3.01	3.11†	2.37	11.6
West	.99	.99	.98*	1.13†	.99	15.7
(21) Az, Co, Id, NM, Ut, Nv, Wy, Mt, Ak	2.25*	2.43	2.62	3.15†	2.40	9.0
(22) Wa, Or, Hi	1.37*	1.47	1.58	2.14†	1.46	4.3
(23) Ca	.22*	.26	.34†	.33	.26	2.4
United States	1.32	1.28*	1.35	1.37†	1.30	118.8

according to Table 5.7, only the South receives positive net transfers from NIT, while the other regions incur net liabilities. In Table 5.9, however, all but one of the regions show *positive* indicators of induced employment, although the indicators of the southern regions do tend to be higher than the national indicator.[9] In effect, then, the indirect impacts of the program—operating through induced consumption and production decisions—tend to reduce the substantial advantage conveyed to the low-income (primarily southern) regions by the allocation of net transfers. While net transfers are concentrated on particular low-income regions, the program-induced creation of jobs tends to be spread more evenly across the nation.

This spreading effect caused by the induced consumption and production adjustments is reflected in the smaller range of regional impact indicators for induced employment than for net transfers. For FAP, the regional impact indicators for net transfers (Table 5.7) range from 29.6 (Mississippi) to −3.3 (New York). The indicators of induced employment (Table 5.8) show a much narrower range—from 18.2 (Mississippi) to −.9 (New York). For NIT, the regional impact indicators for net transfers (Table 5.7) range from 24.0 (Mississippi) to −2.2 (New York), while the range of regional indicators of induced employment (Table 5.9) extends from 15.0 (Mississippi) to −.3 (New York).

These comparisons suggest that the final effects on income distribution of the redistributive policies examined (FAP and NIT) are likely to be weaker than they seem from the initial distribution of net transfers. While transferring income from higher to lower income classes (or from higher-income to lower-income regions) achieves some net reduction in inequality, the consumption and production decisions induced by the initial transfers tend to offset the first-round (or intended) redistribution. The employment induced by the policy tends to be heavily concentrated, compared to the preprogram distribution of employment, among the high-skill, high-wage classes. As a result, the indirect effects of the programs tend to shift the structure of employment away from low-skill, low-earnings classes and toward high-skill, high-earnings classes.

In the final set of estimates from the income distribution module, the effect of program-induced labor demands, by earnings class, on the distribution of family income is derived. As indicated earlier, these estimates are based on the assumption that the mean increase in induced

---

[9]For the FAP analysis, only 4 of the 11 nonsouthern regions have indicators higher than that of the nation (1.35), while 9 of the 12 southern regions do.

earnings in a regional earnings class accrues to each earner in that regional earnings class.[10]

In Table 5.10, the distribution of program-induced earnings by family income class is shown for the four census regions and the United States, for both FAP and NIT. This distribution is compared with the distributions of (1) total earned income prior to the program, (2) total family income prior to the program, and (3) total family income prior to the program plus net transfers. As expected, the distribution of program-induced earnings is less heavily concentrated on low-income classes than is either total preprogram income or total preprogram income plus net transfers. For the nation as a whole, 4.5 percent of the policy-induced earnings accrues to families with less than $5000 of income, while 5.7 percent of total family income and 6.1 percent of total family income plus net transfers accrue to such families. Somewhat surprisingly, the highest income class (more than $10,000) receives a *smaller* share—75 percent—of program-induced earnings than of either preprogram family income or preprogram family income plus net transfers (78 percent in both cases). Hence, when program-induced earnings increments are allocated to income classes according to our assumption, middle-income families ($5000–$10,000) gain relative to higher-income or lower-income families.

When the distribution of program-induced earnings is compared to the distribution of preprogram earnings, another somewhat unexpected pattern appears. Whereas induced labor demands, relative to preprogram employment, are concentrated in high earnings classes, the distribution of induced earnings *by family income class* is slightly more favorable to the poor than the distribution of preprogram earnings. For the entire United States, families with less than $5000 of income receive about 2.6 percent of preprogram earnings, compared to 4.5 percent of the earnings induced by either FAP or NIT. This alteration of the distribution has two sources. The first is the prevalence of part-time, part-year (secondary) workers among households in the low earnings classes. Even though workers in these earnings classes experience smaller employment increments than those in higher earnings classes, the combined income of their family units is, in some cases, higher than that of families

---

[10]Because of the arbitrary—and, as will be pointed out later, extreme—nature of this assumption, these results should be interpreted with caution. The large range of possible assumptions, combined with the relatively small increment to earnings ($730 million to $760 million) and the substantial cost of estimating the effect of alternative assumptions, have lead us to calculate and display the implications of this assumption only.

TABLE 5.10

Percentage distribution of induced earnings, preprogram earnings, preprogram family income, and preprogram income plus net transfers, for FAP and NIT, by family income class and by region

	FAP			NIT		
	Less than $5000	$5000–$10,000	More than $10,000	Less than $5000	$5000–$10,000	More than $10,000
Northeast						
Induced earnings	3.9	16.4	79.7	0.1	15.3	84.6
Preprogram earnings	1.8	13.1	85.1	1.8	13.1	85.1
Preprogram income	4.7	14.9	80.4	4.7	14.9	80.4
Preprogram income plus net transfers	4.9	15.0	80.1	4.9	15.0	80.1
North Central						
Induced earnings	3.3	19.6	77.1	3.0	18.4	78.6
Preprogram earnings	2.2	14.1	83.7	2.2	14.1	83.7
Preprogram income	5.2	15.6	79.2	5.2	15.6	79.2
Preprogram income plus net transfers	5.6	15.0	79.4	5.6	15.6	78.9
South						
Induced earnings	5.7	22.7	71.6	5.6	23.0	71.4
Preprogram earnings	3.9	19.4	76.7	3.9	19.4	76.7
Preprogram income	7.3	19.2	73.5	7.3	19.2	73.5
Preprogram income plus net transfers	8.0	19.0	73.0	8.0	19.0	73.0
West						
Induced earnings	3.3	16.4	80.3	3.5	19.4	77.1
Preprogram earnings	2.4	13.3	84.3	2.4	13.3	84.3
Preprogram income	5.4	14.4	80.2	5.4	14.4	80.2
Preprogram income plus net transfers	5.5	14.4	80.1	5.8	14.4	79.8
United States						
Induced earnings	4.6	20.9	74.4	4.5	19.9	75.6
Preprogram earnings	2.6	14.9	82.5	2.6	14.9	82.5
Preprogram income	5.7	16.2	78.1	5.7	16.2	78.1
Preprogram income plus net transfers	6.1	16.2	77.7	6.1	16.2	77.7

in higher earnings classes. Because of this "leapfrogging," *families* in lower *income* classes tend to receive larger increments to earnings than those suggested by the distribution of *individual* incremental employment by *earnings* class.

The second source of this unexpected alteration in the distribution is related to the first and is attributable to our assumption regarding the allocation of earnings increments among individuals. Because the average earnings increment in an earnings class is assigned to each earner in the class, part-year, part-time workers receive *larger* increases relative to their earnings than do full-time, full-year workers. And, because of (1) the greater prevalence of part-time, part-year workers in the lower earnings classes and (2) the general tendency for those with low earnings to be associated with low income classes, the magnitude of this effect tends to be greater in lower than in higher income classes. The effect of this second source, then, magnifies that of the first source of the altered distribution.[11]

With few exceptions, the pattern for the nation is replicated in each of the regions. In nearly all cases,[12] the distribution of the induced earnings increment is more favorable to the poor than the distribution of preprogram earnings but substantially less favorable to the poor than the distribution of either preprogram income or preprogram income plus net transfers. And in all regions, program-induced earnings increments favor the $5000–$10,000 income class more than do any of the other earnings or income distributions. If, in fact, the earnings increment is distributed among workers the way we have assumed it is, the program will tend to narrow the distributions of earnings and total income by income class—the center of the distribution will tend to receive a share of program-generated income greater than its share of either preprogram earnings or preprogram income. Again, this result must be interpreted with caution—the earnings increment is not large relative to preprogram income, and the result is sensitive to the assumed distribution of earnings increments among workers.

[11] If the regional distributions of occupational earnings had been based on full-time, full-year workers rather than on all earners and if the earnings increments had been allocated among either full-time, full-year workers or primary earners in a family, both sources of the alteration would have been reduced and the distribution of impacts by *income* class would have more closely approximated the distribution of impacts by *earnings* class.

[12] The only exception is the Northeast for the NIT simulation.

6

Between first-round and final income redistribution: The process of economic adjustment

As Chapter 5 indicated, between the first-round distribution of transfers and taxes and the ultimate distributional impact of tax–transfer policy lie an enormous number of economic decisions and adjustments. The nature of these adjustments determines the extent to which the ultimate redistribution of income induced by the policy will be greater or smaller than the first-round impacts. This chapter analyzes the nature of the adjustments in consumption expenditures, gross output, and employment induced by the Family Assistance Plan (FAP) and a negative income tax (NIT). These adjustments determine the effects on the distributions of earnings and final income described in the previous chapter.

Effects of FAP and NIT on consumption expenditures

In empirically implementing the consumption expenditure module, four simulations are undertaken. In Table 6.1, the combinations of programs and household expenditure systems that define these simulations are indicated. While only the current-income approach is simulated for FAP, the current-income approach and both variants of the normal-income approach are simulated for NIT.

TABLE 6.1

Program variants and consumption expenditure approaches simulated

Program	Current income, marginal budget shares	Normal income, average budget shares	Normal income, marginal budget shares
FAP	I	—	—
NIT	II	III	IV

Effects of gross transfers on consumption, by industry and region

In Table 6.2, the predicted expenditures generated by *gross* transfers are shown for the major production sectors. The results of Simulations I and II make possible comparisons between the two transfer programs. Because the same consumption model, based on current income, underlies both of these simulations, the sectoral differences between them are attributable only to differences in the distribution of benefits and in the relative size of the two programs.[1] Both FAP and NIT gross transfers generate approximately $3.7 billion of consumption expenditures. Induced consumption is 112 percent of gross transfers for FAP and about 109 percent for NIT, reflecting differences in the distribution of benefits by income class.[2]

In percentage terms, the sectoral impact of the final demands is nearly identical for the two transfer programs. In both cases, the bulk of the demands (66–67 percent) is imposed on the manufacturing sector; over two-thirds of these demands are concentrated in nondurable goods manufacturing. The service industries account for an additional 30 percent of the total demand from the two programs. The detailed sectors receiving the largest impacts are food and kindred products (about 21 percent in both simulations), motor vehicles (about 9 percent), and medical and educational services (about 11 percent).

The third column in each of the simulation panels shows the ratio of the percentage of incremental demand in a sector to the percentage of total national consumption demand accounted for by that sector.[3]

---

[1] These two simulations based on current income form the basis for the distributional analysis of Chapter 5.

[2] As described in Chapter 4, the marginal propensity to spend of very low-income families is estimated to be greater than unity in the current-income expenditure model. Because the bulk of gross transfer benefits from both FAP and NIT accrues to such families, total induced expenditures are estimated to exceed gross transfers.

[3] The percentage distribution of national consumption expenditures is shown in the first column of the table.

Any production sector with a ratio greater than unity will increase its share of total national consumption because of gross transfers; the size of the ratio indicates the extent of relative gain or loss. The major sectors with the largest relative gains are mining (a ratio of 5.70), durable goods manufacturing (1.52), and nondurable goods manufacturing (1.14). Interestingly, the service sector is a relative loser, with a ratio of .76. While the transportation sector has a ratio of 1.18, wholesale and retail trade has a very low ratio of .05.[4] Among the detailed industries, the largest relative gainers are petroleum and related products (1.90), motor vehicles (1.81), and medical and educational services (1.34).

These comparisons provide some insight into the final distributional impact of the gains in earnings among high-skill, high-wage workers that were observed in Chapter 5. Among the detailed sectors receiving the largest incremental demands (those with ratios substantially greater than unity) are the petroleum, motor vehicle, finance and insurance, and medical and educational sectors. All of these sectors employ large numbers of relatively high-skill, high-wage workers. On the other hand, those sectors that employ high concentrations of low-skill, low-wage workers (agriculture, food products, apparel, and wholesale and retail trade) receive relatively small incremental demands from the programs. For both FAP and NIT, the impact ratios for these sectors are below unity. In short, the consumption demands induced by the gross transfers tend to involve sectors that employ relatively high concentrations of high-skill, high-wage workers.

While Simulations I and II yield comparisons between the two types of transfer programs (holding constant the household expenditure system), Simulations II, III, and IV allow comparison of the effects of different assumptions regarding consumption behavior, holding program constant. While Simulation II bases household expenditures on current income and marginal budget shares, Simulations III and IV presume that household expenditures are based on normal income. While Simulation III allocates the induced change in expenditures according to preprogram budget shares, Simulation IV uses marginal budget shares.

As a result of these different assumptions regarding consumption behavior, the estimates of the total expenditures induced by gross transfers vary. Simulation II projects an increase in consumption of $3.7 billion, or 109 percent of gross transfers; the comparable figures for

---

[4]As indicated earlier, this result is due to our definition of detailed consumption categories in moving from the Consumer Expenditure Survey to the 56 input–output categories. See Appendix E.

TABLE 6.2
Change in consumption expenditures induced by gross transfers of FAP and NIT, by industry

Production sector	Percentage distribution of national consumption	Simulation I[a] (FAP)			Simulation II[b] (NIT)		
		Change in consumption (in millions of dollars)	Percentage of change in total consumption	Ratio of percentage of change in consumption to percentage of total national consumption	Change in consumption (in millions of dollars)	Percentage of change in total consumption	Ratio of percentage of change in consumption to percentage of total national consumption
Agriculture, forestry, and fisheries	2.51	15.5	.42	.17	16.4	.44	.18
Mining	.10	21.2	.57	5.70	21.3	.57	5.74
Mining, coal	.10	21.2	.57	5.70	21.3	.57	5.74
Manufacturing	54.50	2500.2	66.97	1.23	2465.2	66.39	1.22
Nondurables	41.75	1778.2	47.65	1.14	1741.1	46.89	1.12
Food and kindred products	20.62	792.6	21.24	1.03	769.2	20.71	1.00
Apparel	5.97	184.0	4.93	.83	187.7	5.05	.85
Petroleum and related products	4.67	331.1	8.87	1.90	318.4	8.58	1.84
Other	10.49	470.5	12.61	1.20	465.8	12.54	1.20

Durables	12.75	722.0	19.32	1.52	724.1	19.50	1.53
Motor vehicles	5.24	353.1	9.46	1.81	346.5	9.33	1.78
Other	7.51	368.9	9.89	1.32	377.6	10.17	1.35
Transportation and warehousing	1.65	72.4	1.94	1.18	76.7	2.07	1.25
Wholesale and retail trade	2.37	4.1	.11	.05	3.9	.10	.04
Services	39.41	1119.3	30.00	.76	1129.7	30.42	.77
Electricity, gas, water, and sanitation	3.09	47.8	1.28	.41	46.2	1.24	.40
Finance and insurance	4.60	207.3	5.56	1.21	216.0	5.82	1.26
Real estate and rental	14.70	82.7*	2.22	.15	90.1**	2.43	.17
Medical and educational services, nonprofit organizations	8.07	404.7	10.84	1.34	405.3	10.92	1.35
Other	8.95	376.8	10.01	1.12	372.2	10.02	1.12
Total		3732.7			3713.2		

(Continued)

TABLE 6.2 continued

Production sector	Simulation III[c] (NIT)			Simulation IV[d] (NIT)		
	Change in consumption (in millions of dollars)	Percentage of change in total consumption	Ratio of percentage of change in consumption to percentage of total national consumption	Change in consumption (in millions of dollars)	Percentage of change in total consumption	Ratio of percentage of change in consumption to percentage of total national consumption
Agriculture, forestry, and fisheries	127.3	3.72	1.48	15.1	.50	.20
Mining	9.6	.28	2.80	2.9	.10	.98
Mining, coal	9.6	.28	2.80	2.9	.10	.98
Manufacturing	2145.1	62.70	1.15	1812.4	60.29	1.11
Nondurables	1764.3	51.57	1.24	1310.0	43.58	1.04
Food and kindred products	945.1	27.62	1.34	546.5	18.18	.88
Apparel	256.3	7.49	1.26	233.8	7.78	1.30
Petroleum and related products	138.8	4.06	.87	177.2	5.89	1.26
Other	424.0	12.39	1.18	325.5	11.73	1.12
Durables	380.8	11.13	.87	502.4	16.71	1.31
Motor vehicles	147.8	4.32	.82	753.4	8.43	1.61
Other	233.0	6.81	.91	248.9	8.28	1.10

Transportation and warehousing	35.6	1.04	.63	45.0	1.50	.91
Wholesale and retail trade	4.6	.14	.06	2.9	.10	.04
Services	1099.2	32.13	.82	1127.5	37.51	.95
Electricity, gas, water, and sanitation	152.6	4.46	1.44	93.8	3.12	1.01
Finance and insurance	151.9	4.44	.97	170.2	5.66	1.23
Real estate and rental	317.8***	9.29	.63	158.8****	5.28	.36
Medical and educational services, nonprofit organizations	219.1	6.40	.79	347.0	11.54	1.43
Other	257.8	7.53	.84	357.8	11.90	1.33
Total	3421.4			3005.9		

*Includes 35.7 for maintenance and repair construction.
**Includes 59.3 for maintenance and repair construction.
***Includes 28.4 for maintenance and repair construction.
****Includes 14.7 for maintenance and repair construction.
[a]Simulation I estimates the final consumption demand from the gross transfers (federal benefit payments plus state supplements minus AFDC payments) of FAP, using the current income, marginal budget shares approach.
[b]Simulation II estimates the final consumption demand from the gross transfers (federal benefit payments) of NIT, using the current income, marginal budget shares approach.
[c]Simulation III estimates the final consumption demand from the gross transfers (federal benefit payments) of NIT, using the normal income, average budget shares approach.
[d]Simulation IV estimates the final consumption demand from the gross transfers (federal benefit payments) of NIT, using the normal income, marginal budget shares approach.

Simulations III and IV are $3.4 billion and 100 percent and $3.0 billion and 88 percent, respectively.

While the sectoral pattern of demand is similar among the three simulations, there are some important differences. First, Simulation III concentrates an even higher proportion of demands on nondurable goods manufacturing than does Simulation II (52 percent relative to 47 percent). The total impacts on the manufacturing sector according to Simulations II and IV are very similar. Second, while the relative impacts on the service sector according to Simulations II and III are very close (about 30–32 percent), the induced demand for services indicated by Simulation IV is substantially greater (38 percent). Third, several substantial differences are observed among the detailed industries. While Simulations II and IV allocate 18–20 percent of induced consumption demand to the food and kindred products industry, Simulation III allocates 28 per cent. This larger share results from the assumed identity of average and marginal budget shares, which is implicit in the consumption model of Simulation III. Other divergences occur in the amounts allocated to the motor vehicles and petroleum sectors and, within the service sector, in the amounts allocated to finance and insurance and to medical and educational services.

In addition to the industrial composition of induced demands, their regional distribution is of interest. While the regional pattern of induced consumption expenditures reflects the regional distribution of gross transfers, the regional variations in marginal propensities and tastes yield somewhat divergent regional patterns of induced consumption demands. Moreover, in Simulations III and IV, the regional distribution of program-induced consumption is based on the change in the *normal* incomes of the region's residents rather than on the change in their *measured* incomes.

In Table 6.3, the regional pattern of consumption expenditures induced by gross transfers is presented for the four combinations of program variants and models. For Simulations I and II, the pattern of induced expenditures by region is similar to the regional pattern of gross benefits described in Chapter 5. The only source of deviation from the regional pattern of gross benefits is the varying regional average marginal propensities to consume. For Simulation I—FAP—this ratio varies from 1.67 in New York to about 1.10 in several regions in the deep South. For Simulation II—NIT—the ratio is approximately 1.08–1.09 in all of the regions, a substantially smaller range that is due to the more uniform impact among regions of NIT as compared to the multi-component FAP program.

In both simulations, the largest induced consumption expenditures appear in the South—46 percent for both FAP and NIT. The Northeast shows the smallest induced expenditures in both Simulations I and II (11 percent and 15 percent, respectively).

This pattern is also reflected in the indicator shown in the fourth column for each simulation. This indicator describes the relationship between the regional pattern of marginal (or induced) household expenditures and the preprogram regional pattern of household expenditures. Any region with a score greater than unity will tend to have a higher proportion of national household expenditures after the program than before. These indicators suggest that the gross transfers from both FAP and NIT will tend to shift national household expenditures to the South. For example, Mississippi's share of induced expenditures from FAP is nearly nine times its share of preprogram national consumption, and its share of induced expenditures from NIT is more than seven times its share of preprogram national consumption. Only the South has indicators greater than unity in both Simulations I and II.

Simulations II, III, and IV depict a range of possible expenditure responses to NIT gross transfers. The methods of estimating expenditures underlying each of these simulations account for the differences among them. Both Simulations III and IV predict smaller absolute and relative impacts on the South and the West than does Simulation II. For example, the South accounts for 35 percent of total induced expenditures in Simulations III and IV, compared to 45 percent in Simulation II. Similarly, Mississippi accounts for 5.5 percent of the change in national household expenditures in Simulation II but for only about 2.8 percent in Simulations III and IV.

These same patterns are reflected in the columns reporting regional marginal propensities to consume (third column under each simulation) and marginal consumption share indicators (fourth column under each simulation). In terms of regional shares of marginal consumption, Simulation II shows the South (with an indicator of 1.64) gaining at the expense of the Northeast (.56), while the North Central region (.85) and the West (.89) are relatively unaffected. Conversely, Simulations III and IV show the South (1.25) gaining at the expense of the West (.87) and the Northeast (.84), with the North Central region (1.0) being relatively unaffected.

These patterns are not unexpected. Because the expenditure-estimating methods based on normal income exclude geographic location as a determinant of normal income, the South and the West are predicted to experience smaller increases in normal income than in

TABLE 6.3
Change in consumption expenditures induced by gross transfers of FAP and NIT, by region

Region	Percentage distribution of national consumption	Simulation I (FAP)				Simulation II (NIT)			
		Change in consumption (in millions of dollars)	Percentage of change in consumption	Ratio of consumption induced by gross transfers to gross transfers	Ratio of percentage of change in consumption to percentage of total national consumption	Change in consumption (in millions of dollars)	Percentage of change in consumption	Ratio of consumption induced by gross transfers to gross transfers	Ratio of percentage of change in consumption to percentage of total national consumption
Northeast	26.40	422.4	11.32	1.23	.43	547.8	14.75	1.09	.56
(1) Ct, Me, Ma, NH, RI, Vt	5.96	142.8	3.83	1.14	.64	146.7	3.95	1.09	.66
(2) NY	11.00	69.0	1.85	1.67	.17	159.2	4.29	1.08	.39
(3) Pa, NJ	9.44	210.6	5.64	1.20	.60	242.0	6.52	1.08	.69
North Central	26.70	752.7	20.17	1.14	.76	843.8	22.72	1.09	.85
(4) Oh, Mi	9.30	141.4	3.79	1.27	.41	233.9	6.30	1.08	.68
(5) In, Il	8.07	228.4	6.12	1.12	.76	225.4	6.07	1.08	.75
(6) Wi, Mn	3.83	121.2	3.25	1.11	.85	137.1	3.69	1.09	.96
(7) Ia, Mo	3.32	145.0	3.89	1.12	1.17	128.9	3.47	1.09	1.05
(8) Ks, Nb, ND, SD	2.18	116.7	3.13	1.09	1.44	118.5	3.19	1.09	1.46

	27.76	1699.8	45.55	1.09	1.64	1688.5	45.47	1.09	1.64
South									
(9) De, DC, Md	2.80	61.7	1.65	1.15	.59	90.2	2.43	1.08	.87
(10) Va, WV	2.72	112.3	3.01	1.11	1.11	104.7	2.82	1.08	1.04
(11) NC	1.98	135.8	3.64	1.07	1.84	124.3	3.35	1.09	1.69
(12) SC	.95	99.2	2.66	1.09	2.80	109.2	2.94	1.09	3.09
(13) Ga	1.93	60.0	1.61	1.42	.83	86.0	2.32	1.08	1.20
(14) Fl	3.06	137.3	3.68	1.06	1.20	128.0	3.45	1.08	1.13
(15) Ky, Tn	2.83	175.2	4.69	1.07	1.66	170.7	4.60	1.09	1.67
(16) Al	1.03	121.9	3.27	1.08	3.17	111.3	3.00	1.09	2.91
(17) Ms	.76	243.8	6.53	1.08	8.59	204.0	5.50	1.09	7.23
(18) Ar, Ok	1.82	90.4	2.42	1.08	1.33	90.8	2.45	1.08	1.34
(19) La	1.96	190.4	5.10	1.08	2.60	178.3	4.80	1.09	2.45
(20) Tx	5.93	271.8	7.28	1.09	1.23	291.0	7.84	1.08	1.32
West	19.15	856.8	22.96	1.11	1.20	633.1	17.05	1.08	.89
(21) Az, Co, Id, NM, Ut, Nv, Wy, Mt, Ak	4.20	211.6	5.67	1.09	1.35	224.4	6.04	1.09	1.44
(22) Wa, Or, Hi	3.25	102.5	2.75	1.13	.85	127.8	3.44	1.08	1.06
(23) Ca	11.70	542.7	14.54	1.11	1.24	280.9	7.50	1.08	.65
United States		3731.7		1.12		3713.2		1.09	

(Continued)

TABLE 6.3 continued

Region	Simulation III (NIT)				Simulation IV (NIT)			
	Change in consumption (in millions of dollars)	Percentage of change in consumption	Ratio of consumption induced by gross transfers to gross transfers	Ratio of percentage of change in consumption to percentage of total national consumption	Change in consumption (in millions of dollars)	Percentage of change in consumption	Ratio of consumption induced by gross transfers to gross transfers	Ratio of percentage of change in consumption to percentage of total national consumption
Northeast	752.1	21.98	.99	.83	668.0	22.22	.88	.84
(1) Ct, Me, Ma, NH, RI, Vt	182.7	5.34	1.01	.90	160.3	5.33	.89	.89
(2) NY	253.6	7.41	.96	.67	229.2	7.63	.87	.69
(3) Pa, NJ	315.8	9.23	1.00	.98	278.5	9.27	.88	.98
North Central	909.1	26.57	.99	1.00	791.1	26.32	.86	.99
(4) Oh, Mi	292.2	8.54	.99	.92	253.9	8.45	.86	.91
(5) In, Il	262.5	7.67	.99	.95	228.6	7.61	.86	.94
(6) Wi, Mn	141.3	4.13	.98	1.08	120.1	3.99	.83	1.04
(7) Ia, Mo	116.8	3.41	.99	1.03	101.8	3.39	.87	1.02
(8) Ks, Nb, ND, SD	96.3	2.81	.99	1.29	86.7	2.88	.89	1.32

South	1191.5	34.82	1.02	1.25	1049.8	34.93	.90	1.26

South	1191.5	34.82	1.02	1.25	1049.8	34.93	.90	1.26
(9) De, DC, Md	92.7	2.71	.99	.97	83.1	2.77	.89	.99
(10) Va, WV	78.4	2.29	.99	.84	68.2	2.27	.86	.83
(11) NC	86.2	2.52	1.02	1.27	73.3	2.44	.87	1.23
(12) SC	58.1	1.70	1.03	1.79	51.1	1.70	.91	1.79
(13) Ga	82.4	2.41	1.01	1.25	70.9	2.36	.87	1.22
(14) Fl	91.6	2.68	1.00	.87	78.7	2.62	.86	.86
(15) Ky, Tn	126.5	3.70	1.00	1.31	112.1	3.73	.89	1.32
(16) Al	73.9	2.16	1.04	2.10	65.2	2.17	.91	2.11
(17) Ms	95.2	2.78	1.06	3.66	86.3	2.87	.96	3.78
(18) Ar, Ok	72.6	2.12	1.02	1.17	64.1	2.13	.90	1.17
(19) La	121.3	3.55	1.06	1.81	109.4	3.64	.95	1.86
(20) Tx	212.6	6.21	1.03	1.05	187.4	6.23	.90	1.05
West	568.9	16.63	.99	.87	496.9	16.53	.87	.86
(21) Az, Co, Id, NM, Ut, Nv, Wy, Mt, Ak	174.1	5.09	1.02	1.21	151.8	5.05	.89	1.20
(22) Wa, Or, Hi	100.6	2.94	.99	.90	89.4	2.98	.88	.92
(23) Ca	294.2	8.60	.98	.73	255.7	8.51	.85	.73
United States	3421.6		1.00		3005.8		.88	

current income because of the program. Hence, these regions are expected to show lower shares of national consumption spending in Simulations III and IV than in Simulation II.

Effects of taxes on consumption, by industry and region

As shown in Chapter 5, the costs of financing the transfer programs fall on different groups than do the benefits, the most significant variable determining the incidence of both gains and losses being family income. As a consequence, the size and composition—both by industry and by region—of the impact on household expenditures is substantially different for the tax side of the program than for the transfer side.

Table 6.4 presents the results of simulations designed to estimate the effects on household demand of the increase in tax liabilities necessary to finance FAP and NIT. Simulations I (FAP) and II (NIT) show the same *relative* consumption effects for the various industries, because both the tax structure and the consumption module are identical in the two simulations. These relative effects are indicated in the second and third columns under Simulation I. In both simulations, 54 percent of the reduction in total demand is borne by the manufacturing sector. The service sector experiences 42 percent of the reduction in demand. Both these sectors have preference indicators of approximately unity, indicating that their shares of total national consumption remain unchanged in spite of the increases in taxes required to finance the transfer schemes.

Among the detailed industries, apparel, finance and insurance, and medical and educational services have the largest impact indicators (1.7, 2.3, and 1.8, respectively). These indicators measure *decreases* in consumption caused by the taxes required to finance the programs.

These results provide additional insight into the finding that program-induced increments to earnings are concentrated on high-skill, high-wage workers. Among the larger individual sectors displaying substantial relative decreases in demand are apparel and transportation and warehousing, both of which provide relatively heavy demands for low-skill labor.

Again, Simulations II, III, and IV relate to NIT and yield comparisons among consumption models, holding program constant. While Simulations II and IV have almost identical sector impacts, the impact of Simulation III is substantially different. Relative to Simulations II and IV, Simulation III concentrates its impact far more heavily on the manufacturing sector (61 percent compared to 54 percent) and substantially less heavily on the service sector (35 percent compared to 42 percent).

In Simulation III, the impact indicator for manufacturing is 1.1 (compared to about 1.0 in the other simulations) and the indicator for the service sector falls below unity to .89 (compared to 1.1 in the other simulations).

The regional patterns of consumption changes induced by the financing of the transfer programs are shown in Table 6.5. Because of the regional pattern of tax incidence (see Chapter 5), the regional pattern of consumption is not unexpected. Comparison of the financing of FAP with that of NIT (Simulations I and II) reveals that while the tax-induced reduction in consumption differs slightly between the two programs ($2.07 billion for FAP, $2.13 billion for NIT), the regional distributions of the changed expenditures are identical. The South accounts for about 27 percent of the tax-induced consumption changes; the Northeast and North Central regions account for slightly greater percentages; and the West accounts for about 19 percent. Each of the regions of California, New York, and Pennsylvania–New Jersey experiences more than 10 percent of the expenditure reductions.

As a result of the progressive incidence of taxes, the regional marginal propensities to consume are low. While they exceed unity for all regions in the gross transfer simulations, they range from 61 percent to 66 percent in the tax simulations. For the nation as a whole, the marginal propensity to consume out of transfers is about 1.1 for Simulations I and II; for taxes, the marginal propensity is about .62. These figures indicate that the expenditure increases stimulated by the gross transfers will exceed the expenditure reductions induced by an equivalent amount of taxes, leaving a net increment in aggregate demand.

Simulations II, III, and IV reveal the differential regional effects of applying alternative assumptions regarding expenditure behavior to the same transfer plan—NIT. Although the same amount of tax revenue is raised in all three models, the effects on total consumption expenditures are quite different. In Simulations II and IV, a decrease in consumption spending of approximately $2.1 billion is estimated, implying an average marginal propensity to consume of about .63. In contrast to this, Simulation III estimates a decrease in consumption spending of $3.1 billion, implying a marginal propensity to consume of about .91. The reason for this substantial difference is inherent in the models: Simulations II and IV employ estimated income-specific *marginal* propensities to consume, while Simulation III accepts the *average* propensity to consume of the families in a socioeconomic group as each family's marginal propensity to consume. Overall, however, the pattern of consumption reductions by region does not vary substantially among the simulations.

TABLE 6.4

Change in consumption expenditures induced by taxes required to finance FAP and NIT, by industry

Production sector	Simulation I (FAP)			Simulation II (NIT)		
	Change in consumption (in millions of dollars)	Percentage of change in total consumption	Ratio of percentage of change in consumption to percentage of total national consumption	Change in consumption (in millions of dollars)	Percentage of change in total consumption	Ratio of percentage of change in consumption to percentage of total national consumption
Agriculture, forestry, and fisheries	−26.4	1.27	.51	−27.2	1.27	.51
Mining	−1.6	.08	.80	−1.6	.08	.80
Mining, coal	−1.6	.08	.80	−1.6	.08	.80
Manufacturing	−1112.6	53.73	.99	−1142.5	53.73	.99
Nondurables	−814.4	39.33	.94	−836.1	39.33	.94
Food and kindred products	−379.1	18.31	.89	−389.2	18.31	.89
Apparel	−215.6	10.41	1.74	−221.4	10.41	1.74
Petroleum and related products	−35.1	1.70	.36	−36.1	1.70	.36
Other	−184.6	8.92	.85	−189.5	8.92	.85

Durables	−298.2	14.40	1.13	−306.4	14.40	1.13
Motor vehicles	−116.7	5.64	1.08	−119.9	5.64	1.08
Other	−181.5	8.77	1.17	−186.5	8.77	1.17
Transportation and warehousing	−49.6	2.40	1.45	−51.0	2.40	1.45
Wholesale and retail trade	−1.7	.08	.03	−1.8	.08	.03
Services	−878.7	42.44	1.08	−902.3	42.44	1.08
Electricity, gas, water, and sanitation	−35.1	1.70	.55	−36.0	1.70	.55
Finance and insurance	−221.9	10.72	2.33	−227.9	10.72	2.33
Real estate and rental	−58.7*	2.94	.19	−60.3**	2.94	.19
Medical and educational services, nonprofit organizations	−296.2	14.30	1.77	−304.0	14.30	1.77
Other	−266.8	12.89	1.43	−274.0	12.89	1.43
Total	−2070.7			−2126.3		

(Continued)

TABLE 6.4 continued

Production sector	Simulation III (NIT)			Simulation IV (NIT)		
	Change in consumption (in millions of dollars)	Percentage of change in total consumption	Ratio of percentage of change in consumption to percentage of total national consumption	Change in consumption (in millions of dollars)	Percentage of change in total consumption	Ratio of percentage of change in consumption to percentage of total national consumption
Agriculture, forestry, and fisheries	−81.3	2.62	1.05	−30.1	1.39	.55
Mining	−5.9	.19	1.91	−1.4	.07	.66
Mining, coal	−5.9	.19	1.91	−1.4	.07	.66
Manufacturing	−1879.0	60.61	1.11	−1182.9	54.51	1.00
Nondurables	−1461.5	47.14	1.13	−865.8	39.90	.96
Food and kindred products	−732.5	23.63	1.15	−402.1	18.53	.90
Apparel	−222.4	7.17	1.20	−222.4	10.25	1.72
Petroleum and related products	−146.4	4.72	1.01	−45.5	2.10	.45
Other	−360.2	11.62	1.11	−195.8	9.02	.86

Durables	−417.5	13.47	1.06	−317.0	14.61	1.15
Motor vehicles	−171.5	5.53	1.06	−125.7	5.79	1.11
Other	−246.1	7.94	1.06	−191.3	8.82	1.17
Transportation and warehousing	−44.6	1.44	.87	−50.1	2.31	1.40
Wholesale and retail trade	−3.6	.12	.05	−1.9	.09	.04
Services	−1085.6	35.02	.89	−903.6	41.64	1.06
Electricity, gas, water, and sanitation	−111.4	3.59	1.16	−37.9	1.75	.57
Finance and insurance	−208.8	6.73	1.46	−213.7	9.85	2.14
Real estate and rental	−184.0***	5.94	.40	−75.3****	3.47	.24
Medical and educational services, nonprofit organizations	−270.2	8.71	1.08	−299.5	13.80	1.71
Other	−311.2	10.04	1.12	−277.2	12.77	1.43
Total	−3100.0			−2169.9		

*Includes −21.0 for maintenance and repair construction.
**Includes −31.0 for maintenance and repair construction.
***Includes −37.4 for maintenance and repair construction.
****Includes −26.4 for maintenance and repair construction.

TABLE 6.5

Change in consumption expenditures induced by taxes required to finance FAP and NIT, by region

Region	Simulation I (FAP)				Simulation II (NIT)			
	Change in consumption (in millions of dollars)	Percentage of change in total consumption	Ratio of change in consumption to change in taxes	Ratio of percentage of change in consumption to percentage of total national consumption	Change in consumption (in millions of dollars)	Percentage of change in total consumption	Ratio of change in consumption to change in taxes	Ratio of percentage of change in consumption to percentage of total national consumption
Northeast	−552.3	26.67	.62	1.01	−566.6	26.67	.62	1.01
(1) Ct, Me, Ma, NH, RI, Vt	−118.6	5.73	.62	.96	−121.7	5.73	.62	.96
(2) NY	−220.1	10.63	.61	.97	−225.8	10.63	.61	.97
(3) Pa, NJ	−213.6	10.31	.62	1.09	−219.1	10.31	.62	1.09
North Central	−574.7	27.75	.62	1.04	−589.5	27.75	.62	1.04
(4) Oh, Mi	−216.7	10.47	.62	1.13	−222.3	10.47	.62	1.13
(5) In, Il	−179.4	8.66	.62	1.07	−184.0	8.66	.62	1.07
(6) Wi, Mn	−83.4	4.03	.62	1.05	−85.5	4.03	.62	1.05
(7) Ia, Mo	−57.2	2.76	.63	.83	−58.7	2.76	.63	.83
(8) Ks, Nb, ND, SD	−38.0	1.83	.63	.84	−39.0	1.83	.63	.84

South	−550.8	26.60	.63	.96	−567.2	26.60	.63	.96
(9) De, DC, Md	−70.6	3.41	.61	1.22	−72.4	3.41	.61	1.22
(10) Va, WV	−53.9	2.60	.62	.96	−55.3	2.60	.62	.96
(11) NC	−38.2	1.85	.64	.93	−39.4	1.85	.64	.93
(12) SC	−20.8	1.00	.64	1.05	−21.5	1.00	.64	1.05
(13) Ga	−38.8	1.87	.63	.97	−40.1	1.87	.63	.97
(14) Fl	−74.3	3.59	.62	1.17	−76.3	3.59	.62	1.17
(15) Ky, Tn	−51.4	2.48	.65	.88	−53.1	2.48	.65	.88
(16) Al	−27.4	1.32	.63	1.28	−28.1	1.32	.63	1.28
(17) Ms	−13.9	.67	.66	.88	−14.2	.67	.66	.88
(18) Ar, Ok	−29.8	1.44	.65	.79	−30.6	1.44	.65	.79
(19) La	−26.2	1.27	.65	.65	−26.9	1.27	.65	.65
(20) Tx	−105.5	5.10	.62	.87	−109.3	5.10	.62	.87
West	−393.0	18.98	.62	.99	−403.1	18.98	.62	.99
(21) Az, Co, Id, NM, Ut, Nv, Wy, Mt, Ak	−78.7	3.80	.63	.90	−80.1	3.80	.63	.90
(22) Wa, Or, Hi	−64.1	3.10	.63	.95	−65.7	3.10	.63	.95
(23) Ca	−250.2	12.08	.62	1.03	−257.3	12.08	.62	1.03
United States	−2070.8		.62		−2126.4		.62	

(Continued)

TABLE 6.5 continued

Region	Simulation III (NIT)				Simulation IV (NIT)			
	Change in consumption (in millions of dollars)	Percentage of change in total consumption	Ratio of change in consumption to change in taxes	Ratio of percentage of change in consumption to percentage of total national consumption	Change in consumption (in millions of dollars)	Percentage of change in total consumption	Ratio of change in consumption to change in taxes	Ratio of percentage of change in consumption to percentage of total national consumption
Northeast	−761.4	24.56	.90	.93	−531.9	24.51	.63	.93
(1) Ct, Me, Ma, NH, RI, Vt	−183.3	5.91	.90	.99	−127.7	5.88	.63	.99
(2) NY	−274.4	8.85	.90	.80	−193.0	8.89	.63	.81
(3) Pa, NJ	−303.7	9.80	.90	1.04	−211.2	9.73	.63	1.03
North Central	−852.3	27.50	.91	1.03	−597.3	27.53	.64	1.03
(4) Oh, Mi	−306.2	9.88	.91	1.06	−212.9	9.81	.63	1.06
(5) In, Il	−253.9	8.19	.91	1.02	−178.0	8.20	.64	1.02
(6) Wi, Mn	−132.8	4.28	.91	1.12	−93.1	4.29	.64	1.12
(7) Ia, Mo	−96.7	3.12	.90	.94	−68.5	3.16	.64	.95
(8) Ks, Nb, ND, SD	−62.7	2.02	.90	.93	−44.8	2.07	.65	.95

South	−914.6	29.50	.91	1.06	−639.5	29.47	.63	1.06
(9) De, DC, Md	−91.2	2.94	.91	1.05	−63.3	2.92	.63	1.04
(10) Va, WV	−81.9	2.64	.90	.97	−57.0	2.63	.63	.97
(11) NC	−74.8	2.41	.91	1.22	−51.9	2.39	.63	1.21
(12) SC	−39.9	1.29	.91	1.35	−27.7	1.28	.63	1.34
(13) Ga	−69.7	2.25	.91	1.16	−48.3	2.23	.63	1.15
(14) Fl	−107.0	3.45	.89	1.13	−75.8	3.49	.64	1.14
(15) Ky, Tn	−95.5	3.08	.91	1.09	−66.9	3.08	.64	1.09
(16) Al	−47.1	1.52	.91	1.47	−32.6	1.50	.63	1.46
(17) Ms	−31.8	1.03	.91	1.35	−22.4	1.03	.64	1.36
(18) Ar, Ok	−55.3	1.79	.91	.98	−39.0	1.80	.64	.99
(19) La	−53.6	1.73	.91	.88	−37.8	1.74	.64	.89
(20) Tx	−166.8	5.38	.91	.91	−116.8	5.38	.63	.91
West	−571.7	18.44	.91	.91	−401.3	18.49	.64	.97
(21) Az, Co, Id, NM, Ut, Nv, Wy, Mt, Ak	−132.4	4.27	.91	1.02	−91.7	4.23	.63	1.01
(22) Wa, Or, Hi	−94.3	3.04	.91	.94	−67.0	3.09	.64	.95
(23) Ca	−345.0	11.13	.90	.95	−242.6	11.18	.63	.96
United States	−3100.0		.91		−2170.0		.63	.97

Effects of net transfers on consumption, by industry and region

The *net* effect of the tax–transfer proposals on household expenditures is the sum of the positive effect of the gross transfers and the negative effect of the taxes required to finance the programs. For both programs, this net effect is positive: $1.7 billion for FAP (Simulation I) and $1.6 billion for NIT (Simulation II). This net positive effect is due to the concentration of benefits among low-income households with high marginal consumption propensities and the concentration of the tax burden on higher-income households with lower marginal consumption propensities. Tables 6.6 and 6.7 present the estimates of the industrial and regional composition of the changed consumption demands.

Table 6.6 presents changes in consumption expenditures attributable to the *net* transfers from FAP and NIT, for the major industrial sectors. In all of the simulations, the manufacturing and service sectors experience the largest increments in final demands. In all of the simulations, the increment in expenditures on nondurable goods is more than 50 percent of the total national increment in household expenditures. Indeed, for Simulation III, the increment in expenditures for the nondurable goods sector is nearly as large as the *total* national increment in expenditures.

Simulation I, presenting the results for FAP, projects a $1.4 billion increment in demand for manufacturing as a whole, composed of an increase of $960 million in demand for nondurable goods manufacturing and an increase of $423 million in demand for durable goods manufacturing. The major gainers among the detailed industries are petroleum and motor vehicles, with industrial preference indicators greater than 10.[5] The service sector receives $240 million of new final demand in Simulation I, nearly one-half of it accounted for by medical and educational services. While the industrial preference indicator for the aggregate service sector is 1.7, that for medical and educational services is 3.7. Apparel is the sector experiencing the largest absolute reduction in

---

[5]The industrial preference indicator is the ratio of consumption expenditures generated by the program in an industry to .001 times total 1970 consumption expenditures in the industry (in 1973 dollars). Symbolically,

$$I_i^c = \frac{C_i}{.001 \; (E_i)}$$

where I_i^c is the industrial impact indicator for industry i, C_i is the program-induced change in expenditures in industry i, and E_i is the total 1970 consumption demand in industry i, expressed in 1973 dollars.

demand—a reduction of over $30 million, implying a preference indicator of −1.5. An almost identical pattern is observed in Simulation II (NIT), although the sectoral demands tend to be slightly smaller than those in Simulation I.

These patterns provide further evidence of the economic adjustments that result in the concentration of labor demands on high-skill, high-wage occupations. In both Simulations I and II, for example, the two sectors with preference indicators greater than 10 are petroleum and motor vehicles—both of which tend to have high-skill, high-wage labor forces. On the other hand, the sectors with negative preference indicators (implying net reductions in demand) are agriculture, apparel, and finance and insurance, the first two of which tend to employ large numbers of low-skill, low-wage workers. Moreover, while the food products industry, another relatively low-wage, low-skill industry, has the largest absolute increment to demand of any of the sectors, its preference indicator is only slightly above the total indicator of 4.6. Hence, when both increments and decrements to demand are considered, the *net* consumption expenditure changes induced by FAP and NIT appear to favor sectors that employ high-skill, high-wage workers relative to those that employ low-skill, low-wage workers.

While the general patterns of industrial impacts of Simulations III and IV are similar to those of Simulations I and II, there are a few notable differences. First, Simulation III estimates a much smaller overall impact than do Simulations I and II—$321 million as compared to about $1.6 billion. Second, while manufacturing is a substantial gainer in Simulation III, the durable goods sector experiences a net reduction in final demand. Indeed, net expenditures for nondurable goods are nearly as large as total induced expenditures. Third, the most striking difference in impact between Simulation III and Simulations II and IV occurs in the service sector, which is among the major gainers in the latter two simulations but gains only a trivial $14 million in Simulation III. Fourth, Simulation IV deviates substantially from the general demand pattern of Simulations I and II only in transportation and warehousing, finance and insurance, and apparel. In the transportation and warehousing and finance and insurance sectors, a positive or a slight negative expenditure impact in the first two simulations changes to a substantial negative impact in Simulation IV. The impact on the apparel sector switches from positive in Simulations I and II to negative in Simulation IV.

The net regional impacts of FAP and NIT are shown in Table 6.7. For all of the simulations, the expenditure changes in the South completely dominate those of all other regions.

TABLE 6.6

Change in consumption expenditures induced by net transfers of FAP and NIT, by industry

Production sector	Simulation I (FAP)		Simulation II (NIT)		Simulation III (NIT)		Simulation IV (NIT)	
	Change in consumption (in millions of dollars)	Industrial preference indicator	Change in consumption (in millions of dollars)	Industrial preference indicator	Change in consumption (in millions of dollars)	Industrial preference indicator	Change in consumption (in millions of dollars)	Industrial preference indicator
Agriculture, forestry, and fisheries	−9.9	−1.10	−10.8	−1.20	46.0	5.11	−15.0	−1.66
Mining	19.6	5.20	19.7	5.22	3.7	.97	1.5	.40
Manufacturing	1387.6	7.08	1322.7	6.75	266.1	1.36	629.5	3.21
Nondurables	963.8	6.43	905.0	6.04	302.8	2.02	444.2	2.96
Food and kindred products	413.5	5.58	380.0	5.13	212.6	2.87	144.4	1.95
Apparel	−31.6	−1.47	−33.7	−1.57	34.0	1.58	11.5	.53
Petroleum and related products	296.0	17.64	282.3	16.83	−7.6	−.45	131.6	7.85
Other	285.9	7.58	276.3	7.33	63.8	1.69	156.7	4.15

Durables	423.8	9.24	417.7	9.11	−36.7	−.80	185.3	4.04
Motor vehicles	236.4	12.57	226.6	12.05	−23.7	1.26	127.7	6.79
Other	187.4	6.93	191.1	7.07	−13.0	−.48	57.6	2.13
Transportation and warehousing	22.8	4.80	25.8	5.43	−9.0	−1.89	−5.0	−1.06
Wholesale and retail trade	2.4	.28	2.1	.75	1.0	.12	1.1	.12
Services	240.6	1.69	227.5	1.60	13.6	.10	223.9	1.57
Electricity, gas, water, and sanitation	12.7	1.14	10.1	.91	41.2	3.70	55.9	5.01
Finance and insurance	−14.6	−.88	−11.9	−.72	−56.9	−3.43	−43.5	−2.62
Real estate and rental*	24.0	.45	29.8	.56	133.8	2.51	83.4	1.56
Medical and educational services, nonprofit organizations	108.5	3.74	101.3	3.49	−51.0	−1.76	47.5	1.64
Other	110.0	3.35	98.1	2.99	−53.5	−1.63	80.6	2.46
Total	1663.1	4.62	1586.9	4.41	321.4	.89	836.0	2.33

*Includes maintenance and repair construction.

TABLE 6.7

Change in consumption expenditures induced by net transfers of FAP and NIT, by region

Region	Simulation I (FAP)		Simulation II (NIT)		Simulation III (NIT)		Simulation IV (NIT)	
	Change in consumption (in millions of dollars)	Regional impact indicator	Change in consumption (in millions of dollars)	Regional impact indicator	Change in consumption (in millions of dollars)	Regional impact indicator	Change in consumption (in millions of dollars)	Regional impact indicator
Northeast	−129.9	.91	−18.8	−.13	−9.3	−.06	136.1	.95
(1) Ct, Me, Ma, NH, RI, Vt	24.2	.72	24.9	.75	−.6	−.02	32.6	.97
(2) NY	−151.1	−2.71	−66.6	−1.19	−20.8	−.37	36.2	.65
(3) Pa, NJ	−3.0	−.05	22.9	.38	12.1	.20	67.3	1.12
North Central	176.0	1.24	254.3	1.77	56.8	.39	193.8	1.35
(4) Oh, Mi	−75.3	−1.52	11.6	.23	−14.0	−.28	41.0	.83
(5) In, Il	49.0	1.13	41.4	.95	8.6	.20	50.6	1.16
(6) Wi, Mn	37.8	1.92	51.6	2.62	8.5	.43	27.0	1.37
(7) Ia, Mo	87.8	4.76	70.2	3.81	20.1	1.09	33.3	1.81
(8) Ks, Nb, ND, SD	78.7	6.43	79.5	6.49	33.6	2.74	41.9	3.41

South	1149.0	8.70	1121.3	8.49	276.9	2.10	410.3	3.11
(9) De, DC, Md	-8.9	-.67	17.8	1.34	1.5	.12	19.8	1.50
(10) Va, WV	58.4	4.16	49.4	3.52	-3.5	-.26	11.2	.80
(11) NC	97.6	10.11	84.9	8.79	11.4	1.18	21.4	2.23
(12) SC	78.4	16.53	87.7	18.47	18.2	3.84	23.4	4.93
(13) Ga	21.2	2.40	45.9	5.20	12.7	1.44	22.6	2.56
(14) Fl	63.0	4.26	51.7	3.50	-15.4	-1.04	2.9	.19
(15) Ky, Tn	123.8	8.57	117.6	8.13	31.0	2.15	45.2	3.13
(16) Al	94.5	13.55	83.2	11.94	26.8	3.84	32.6	4.67
(17) Ms	229.9	59.57	189.8	49.18	63.4	16.43	63.9	16.56
(18) Ar, Ok	60.6	6.29	60.2	6.24	17.3	1.79	25.1	2.59
(19) La	164.2	22.69	151.4	20.91	67.7	9.35	71.6	9.89
(20) Tx	166.3	6.75	181.7	7.38	45.8	1.86	70.6	2.87
West	463.8	5.01	230.0	2.48	-2.8	-.03	95.6	1.03
(21) Az, Co, Id, NM, Ut, Nv, Wy, Mt, Ak	132.9	6.32	144.3	6.83	41.7	1.98	60.1	2.85
(22) Wa, Or, Hi	38.4	2.34	62.1	3.77	6.3	.38	22.4	1.37
(23) Ca	292.5	5.29	23.6	.44	-50.8	-.92	13.1	.24
United States	1660.9	3.25	1586.8	3.11	321.6	.63	835.8	1.64

For FAP, the increase in household spending in the South equals 70 percent of the increase in the entire nation. In part, this is due to the *reduction* in consumption of nearly $130 million for the Northeast. Because of the large change in consumption in California (+$293 million), the West shows an increase of nearly $.5 billion. The North Central region shows a net increase of less than $200 million in consumption expenditures.

This pattern is summarized in the column of regional impact indicators. These indicators measure the net effect on final consumption of the tax–transfer programs, relative to the base level of total consumption demand in the region.[6] Of the 23 regions, 14 have regional indicators greater than the national indicator of 3.25; 10 of these 14 regions are in the South. For the entire South, the indicator is 8.70, about 2.7 times the national indicator. The West also has an indicator greater than that of the nation as a whole.

While the net effect of NIT (Simulation II) on household expenditures is roughly similar to that of FAP, the variation among regions is smaller. Under NIT, the Northeast experiences a reduction in spending, but a much smaller reduction than the one projected in Simulation I. The aggregate increase in expenditures in the South is more than four times as large as the increase in any other region; the South's share of the total national increase is again about 70 percent. The North Central and West regions both experience increases in spending of about $250 million. Again the regional impact indicators summarize this pattern. Of the 15 regional indicators greater than the national indicator of 3.11, 11 are in the South.

Simulations III and IV, based on normal income rather than on current income, estimate substantially smaller increases in national household expenditures than the increase estimated in Simulation II for the same transfer plan: $.3 billion and $.8 billion as compared to $1.6 billion in Simulation II. In Simulation III, 6 of the 23 regions show

---

[6]The regional impact indicator is the ratio of dollars of regional net consumption demand generated by the program to .001 times the total 1970 consumption demand in the region (in 1973 dollars). Symbolically,

$$I_r^c = \frac{C_r}{.001 \, (E_r)}$$

where I_r^c is the regional impact indicator for region r, C_r is the program-induced change in consumption expenditures in region r, and E_r is the total 1970 consumption demand in region r, expressed in 1973 dollars.

negative expenditure effects. The South again dominates the other regions in both of these simulations, though it accounts for less than 50 percent of total national spending in Simulation IV.

Effects of FAP and NIT on gross output

Detailing the consumption demands induced by the tax–transfer programs is only an intermediate step in tracing out the full economic impacts of the policies. Because of the shift in the level and composition of consumption expenditures, some industries in some regions experience increased demand while other industries in other regions experience shrinking markets. These first-round spending shifts also affect intermediate demands. As these interdependent demand changes work their way through the economy, the level of gross output in the economy in altered, as well as its regional and industrial composition.

The gross output module traces these interindustry impacts through the economy. In this section, the anatomy of these changes in gross output is presented, first by industry and then by region. Again, the results of four simulations are analyzed; however, unlike the discussion of consumption expenditure changes, this discussion covers only the impacts induced by *net* transfers.

In Table 6.8, the net impact on output of the *net* transfers generated by FAP and NIT is presented for the major industrial sectors and for a limited set of the larger detailed industries. For both FAP (Simulation I) and NIT (Simulation II), nondurable goods manufacturing accounts for a large share—about 28 percent—of the total national increase in gross output. Durable goods manufacturing, wholesale and retail trade, and services together account for another 55 percent of the total. In addition to showing the dollar value of changes in gross output, Table 6.8 presents an industrial impact indicator, which reflects the size of the induced impact on a sector relative to the total size of the sector.[7] The size of this indicator for the nation is 1.7 for FAP and 1.6 for NIT, implying that

---

[7]This indicator, similar to those employed earlier, is defined as

$$I_i^G = \frac{G_i}{.001\,(O_i)}$$

where I_i^G is the industrial impact indicator for industry i, G_i is the program-induced change in gross output in industry i, and O_i is the 1970 gross output in industry i, expressed in 1973 dollars.

TABLE 6.8

Gross output impact generated by net transfers of FAP and NIT, by production sector

Production sector	Simulation I (FAP)		Simulation II (NIT)		Simulation III (NIT)		Simulation IV (NIT)	
	Change in gross output (in millions of dollars)	Industrial gross output impact indicator	Change in gross output (in millions of dollars)	Industrial gross output impact indicator	Change in gross output (in millions of dollars)	Industrial gross output impact indicator	Change in gross output (in millions of dollars)	Industrial gross output impact indicator
Agriculture, forestry, and fisheries	166.8	1.73	158.7	1.65	127.5	1.32	55.0	.51
Livestock and livestock products	79.2	2.01	76.8	1.94	68.6	1.51	24.2	.53
Other agricultural products	75.6	2.06	70.9	1.93	52.4	1.12	26.4	.56
Other agricultural, forestry, and fishing industries	12.0	3.30	10.9	3.00	6.5	1.79	4.3	1.18
Mining	107.0	3.46	101.7	3.29	9.1	.29	50.4	1.63
Construction	47.3	.31	48.0	.31	9.9	.06	23.8	.16
Nondurable manufacturing	883.6	2.43	831.4	2.29	295.7	.81	412.8	1.14
Food and kindred products	361.1	3.14	333.2	2.90	185.2	1.50	127.4	1.03
Other nondurable manufacturing	522.5	2.17	498.2	2.07	110.5	.46	285.5	1.19

Durable manufacturing	651.7	1.72	632.2	1.67	−31.7	−.08	306.3	.81
Primary iron and steel	61.0	1.50	58.3	1.43	−.4	−.01	30.4	.76
Motor vehicles, equipment	292.3	5.20	279.7	4.97	−30.7	−.46	161.0	2.39
Other durable manufacturing	298.4	1.10	294.2	1.08	−.5	−.00	114.9	.42
Transportation and warehousing	128.5	2.02	127.1	2.00	10.7	.17	39.5	.62
Wholesale and retail trade	585.4	2.92	559.0	2.79	125.1	.62	263.0	1.31
Services	540.9	1.00	510.1	.94	59.2	.11	373.7	.69
Electricity, gas, water, and sanitation	63.1	1.31	57.4	1.19	56.1	1.28	92.1	2.10
Finance and insurance	17.9	.29	19.7	.32	−60.2	−1.04	−34.4	−.60
Real estate and rental	95.5	.38	94.7	.38	151.3	1.17	123.8	.96
Medical and educational services, nonprofit organizations	112.2	1.80	104.9	1.68	−51.4	−.91	48.7	.86
Other	252.2	1.24	233.4	1.15	−36.6	−.18	143.6	.71
Total	3111.0	1.71	2968.1	1.63	605.6	.33	1524.6	.84

the total program-induced change in national output is equal to about two-tenths of one percent of gross output. Any industry with an indicator greater than the national indicator experiences a larger increase in gross output than does the nation as a whole; any industry with a smaller indicator is less affected than the nation as a whole. The major sectors with the largest relative impacts are mining, with an indicator of from 3.3 to 3.5; nondurable goods manufacturing, with an indicator of from 2.3 to 2.4; and wholesale and retail trade, with an indicator of from 2.8 to 2.9. The service sector experiences a smaller impact than the nation as a whole; it has an indicator of from .9 to 1.0.

These aggregate sectors, however, disguise significant variation among the more detailed industries. For example, within the durable goods manufacturing sector, whose overall indicator is 1.7, the motor vehicles industry has an indicator of about 5.0. Similarly, while the entire service sector has an indicator of 1.0 or less, the indicator for medical and educational services is nearly 2.0.

Again Simulation IV for NIT shows an impact pattern similar to that of Simulation II, even though the Simulation IV aggregate national impact, $1.5 billion, is only about one-half that of Simulation II. The most significant difference is in the finance and insurance sector, for which the Simulation II estimate of $20 million becomes −$34 million in Simulation IV.

Simulation III, however, predicts a radically different pattern of total impact and industrial impact than Simulations II and IV. The total estimated change in output of Simulation III is only $.6 billion, of which the vast bulk is concentrated in agriculture, forestry, and fisheries and nondurable goods manufacturing. Between them, these two sectors account for two-thirds of the nation's total change in output. Several of the major sectors and a number of the detailed industries show negative impacts on gross output.

Additional information about the adjustments that contribute to the concentration of labor demands on high-skill, high-wage workers can be gained through examination of the detailed industrial pattern of gross outputs induced by the net transfers.[8] For both the FAP and NIT simulations, a number of industries that are substantial employers of low-skill, low-wage workers have either negative or very low increases in gross output. For example, while the overall impact indicator for the

---

[8]The full list of detailed industries, together with the gross output impact indicators from the net transfers of FAP (Simulation I) and NIT (Simulation II) is presented in Appendix K.

FAP simulation is 1.71, the industries of fabric, apparel, footwear and leather products, stone and clay products, and hotels and repair services except auto—all substantial employers of low-wage labor—have impact indicators of .13, −.78, .36, .54, and −.47. Taken together, these sectors are projected to incur a *negative* increment to gross output demand, and hence to labor demand, because of FAP. Conversely, a number of sectors that employ relatively large numbers of high-skill, high-wage workers experience very large increases in gross output. They include crude petroleum and natural gas (with an impact indicator of 4.29), petroleum and related industry (5.26), motor vehicles (5.20), and auto repair services (5.34). Together, these industries account for nearly 25 percent of the total national increment to gross output of $3.1 billion. A very similar pattern exists for Simulation II (NIT). While this evidence is not conclusive, it does suggest that as low-income families spend more and high-income families spend less because of the program, the demand shifts that occur work to the disadvantage of those sectors that are the largest providers of jobs for low-skill, low-wage workers.

Table 6.9 presents the regional distribution of the gross outputs generated by FAP and NIT. In Simulations I and II, industries in the South are estimated to experience an increase in output of $1.6 billion—more than one-half of that for the entire nation. In Simulation I, the Northeast experiences a very small positive change in gross output ($23 million); this is explained in part by a reduction in output in New York, the only detailed region experiencing a decrease in gross output. In Simulation II, the Northeast fares much better—an impact of $150 million—even though New York again experiences a reduction in output. The North Central region and the West experience substantially larger impacts than the Northeast in Simulations I and II.

For FAP, five detailed regions show production increases of more than $200 million: one in the North Central region, three in the South, and one—California—in the West. California's output increases by more than $400 million, the largest increase for a detailed region. For NIT, three regions experience increases of more than $200 million: two in the North Central region and one in the South. In this simulation, Ohio–Michigan sustains the greatest impact, more than $265 million, while California's increase is less than $100 million.

These estimates of total impact on gross output can be misleading because of the wide variation in industrial capacity among the regions. For example, the total preprogram production of New York is nearly 15 times that of Mississippi. To adjust for this, Table 6.9 presents a regional impact indicator that suggests the relationship of the output induced

TABLE 6.9
Gross output impact generated by net transfers of FAP and NIT, by region

Region	Simulation I (FAP)		Simulation II (NIT)		Simulation III (NIT)		Simulation IV (NIT)	
	Change in gross output (in millions of dollars)	Regional gross output impact indicator	Change in gross output (in millions of dollars)	Regional gross output impact indicator	Change in gross output (in millions of dollars)	Regional gross output impact indicator	Change in gross output (in millions of dollars)	Regional gross output impact indicator
Northeast	23.5	.05	150.1	.32	20.1	.04	246.3	.52
(1) Ct, Me, Ma, NH, RI, Vt	42.3	.42	48.6	.48	6.1	.06	50.1	.50
(2) NY	−108.4	−.49	−24.8	−.11	−9.3	−.04	66.4	.30
(3) Pa, NJ	89.6	.51	126.3	.72	23.3	.13	129.8	.74
North Central	832.5	1.44	905.0	1.57	173.7	.30	525.2	.91
(4) Oh, Mi	178.4	.88	265.3	1.31	−23.1	−.11	188.8	.93
(5) In, Il	215.9	1.26	210.5	1.23	44.7	.26	135.0	.79
(6) Wi, Mn	117.9	1.52	131.9	1.70	34.0	.44	64.0	.83
(7) Ia, Mo	190.3	2.61	169.9	2.33	57.5	.79	76.7	1.05
(8) Ks, Nb, ND, SD	130.0	2.66	127.2	2.60	60.5	1.24	60.8	1.24

South	1616.0	3.40	1570.9	3.31	398.9	.84	617.7	1.30
(9) De, DC, Md	21.2	.48	43.3	.98	3.7	.08	30.7	.70
(10) Va, WV	86.7	1.79	78.4	1.62	3.3	.07	25.7	.53
(11) NC	144.1	3.47	134.0	3.23	27.5	.66	48.4	1.17
(12) SC	76.8	4.23	83.6	4.60	22.1	1.22	26.6	1.47
(13) Ga	53.9	1.55	75.4	2.17	19.9	.57	32.1	.92
(14) Fl	62.6	1.60	53.0	1.35	-10.8	-.28	4.6	.11
(15) Ky, Tn	199.4	3.92	186.5	3.67	57.8	1.14	76.5	1.50
(16) Al	101.7	4.25	91.7	3.83	31.7	1.32	37.0	1.55
(17) Ms	228.0	17.84	189.8	14.85	66.3	5.19	66.1	5.17
(18) Ar, Ok	101.2	3.09	97.1	2.96	31.6	.96	41.2	1.26
(19) La	236.5	6.97	220.3	6.49	80.8	2.38	99.8	2.94
(20) Tx	303.9	3.23	317.7	3.38	64.9	.69	129.1	1.37
West	639.1	2.09	342.1	1.12	13.0	.04	135.3	.44
(21) Az, Co, Id, NM, Ut, Nv, Wy, Mt, Ak	162.4	2.11	165.2	2.15	49.8	.65	68.3	.89
(22) Wa, Or, Hi	63.9	1.22	80.3	1.53	11.0	.21	26.1	.50
(23) Ca	412.8	2.16	96.6	.51	-47.8	-.25	40.8	.21
United States	3111.0	1.71	2968.1	1.63	605.6	.33	1524.6	.84

by the program in a region to the region's existing industrial output.[9] For the nation as a whole, this indicator is 1.7 for FAP and 1.6 for NIT. For FAP, the indicator ranges from 17.8 (Mississippi) to −.5 (New York). The range in the NIT simulation is from 14.9 (Mississippi) to −.1 (New York). As the table indicates, the southern regions generally have significantly larger indicators than most of the other detailed regions or the nation as a whole. Of the 10 regions with impact indicators greater than 2.5 in Simulation I, 8 are in the South; of the 9 regions with indicators greater than 2.5 in Simulation II, 8 are in the South. In Simulation I, 3 of the 4 regions with the lowest indicators are in the Northeast; in Simulation II, the regions with the lowest indicators are New York, New England, and California. The large relative gains by the southern and rural regions, noted earlier, are again borne out in these simulations. The high-income and urban regions of the Northeast and West are the relative losers.

Simulations III and IV estimate the effects of NIT, calculating expenditures on the basis of normal income rather than current income. While Simulation IV projects an impact on national gross output of $1.5 billion, the estimate for Simulation III is a very small $.6 billion. The general pattern of regional impacts in Simulation IV is similar to that in Simulation II, but with a smaller variance among regions. While the South again dominates, the North Central region also has an impact indicator above the national indicator.

Simulation III estimates a pattern of regional impacts that is substantially different from those in the other simulations. Four of the regions (Florida, California, New York, and Ohio–Michigan) show negative changes in gross output, while the largest positive impact accrues to Louisiana. Again, however, the bulk of the national impact falls in the South and in nonsouthern rural regions. The Northeast and West experience negligible impacts of $20 million and $13 million. As shown by the regional impact indicator, the relative impact is substantially greater on the South than on the other regions—of the six detailed regions with indicators of 1.0 or more, five are in the South.

---

[9]This indicator is expressed symbolically as

$$I_r^G = \frac{G_r}{.001 (O_r)}$$

where I_r^G is the regional impact indicator for region r, G_r is the program-induced change in gross output in region r, and O_r is the 1970 gross output in region r, expressed in 1973 dollars.

TABLE 6.10

Ratios of gross output to consumption expenditures generated by net transfers of FAP and NIT, by major region

Region	Simulation I (FAP)	Simulation II (NIT)
Northeast	*	*
North Central	4.7	3.6
South	1.4	1.4
West	1.4	1.5
United States	1.9	1.9

*This ratio cannot be calculated, as consumption expenditures were negative in both Simulation I (−$130 million) and Simulation II (−$19 million). Gross output, however, was $24 million in Simulation I and $150 million in Simulation II.

One final point is worth noting. While the impact on gross output in the South is substantial, the South's share of total program-induced gross output is not as great as its share of either net transfers or consumption spending. There is significant leakage of generated demands out of both the South and the West. The extent of this leakage is indicated in Table 6.10, which shows, for Simulations I (FAP) and II (NIT), the ratio of gross output (from Table 6.9) to consumption expenditures (from Table 6.7) for each of the major regions and for the nation. In both simulations, the ratio of gross output to consumption expenditures is 1.9 for the nation but only about 1.4 for the South and the West. For the North Central region, however, the ratio is greater than 3.5 in both simulations. As a result of the interindustry relationships, then, a substantial share of second-, third-, and nth-round demands falls on industries whose production occurs in the North Central region. To some extent the high concentration of net transfers in certain regions—apparently a reflection of the redistributional intent of policymakers—is eroded in the process of consumption and production. The stimulation of economic activity in the regions that receive large net transfers is substantially smaller than the initial redistributive pattern would lead one to predict.

Effects of FAP and NIT on labor demand

The pattern of changes in gross outputs implies subsequent changes in the demand for primary inputs—labor and capital. In the factor employment module of the simulation model, patterns of induced demands for labor inputs are estimated under varying assumptions.

TABLE 6.11
Labor demands induced by net transfers of FAP and NIT, by occupation

Occupations	Simulation I (FAP)		Simulation II (NIT)		Simulation III (NIT)		Simulation IV (NIT)	
	Change in labor demand (in thousands of man years)	Occupational impact indicator	Change in labor demand (in thousands of man years)	Occupational impact indicator	Change in labor demand (in thousands of man years)	Occupational impact indicator	Change in labor demand (in thousands of man years)	Occupational impact indicator
Professional, technical, and kindred	13.9	1.06	13.5	1.03	−1.9	−.15	6.4	.49
Managers, officials, and proprietors	15.3	1.69	14.7	1.62	1.4	.15	6.1	.67
Sales workers	13.2	2.24	12.7	2.15	2.2	.38	5.4	.91
Clerical and kindred	20.9	1.42	20.1	1.37	.1	.01	7.9	.54
Stenographers, typists, and secretaries	4.8	1.24	4.7	1.20	−.4	−.10	1.8	.46
Bookkeepers and accounting clerks	2.3	1.65	2.2	1.59	.1	.09	.8	.62
Others	13.8	1.41	13.3	1.40	.4	.04	5.3	.56

Craftsmen, foremen, and kindred	15.6	1.37	15.1	1.33	1.8	.16	7.4	.65
Construction craftsmen	4.7	1.00	4.6	.99	.8	.18	2.1	.45
Metalworking craftsmen	1.5	1.27	1.4	1.19	.0	.00	.7	.59
Printing trade craftsmen	.3	.98	.3	.86	-.0	-.06	.1	.46
Transportation, public utility, mechanics and repairmen	6.7	2.73	6.4	2.62	.6	.26	3.4	1.40
Other craftsmen	2.4	1.71	2.3	1.66	.4	.26	1.1	.76
Operatives and kindred	23.7	1.60	22.8	1.54	5.6	.38	11.3	.76
Drivers, bus, truck, and tractor	4.4	1.89	4.3	1.86	.8	.34	1.7	.73
Textile operatives	-.1	-.11	-.2	-.18	.9	1.03	.5	.52
Others	19.4	2.59	18.7	2.49	3.9	.52	9.1	1.21
Laborers except farm	5.4	1.42	5.2	1.39	1.2	.33	2.4	.64
Service workers	12.0	.91	11.5	.87	-.5	-.04	5.1	.39
Food service workers	5.7	2.14	5.5	2.05	.8	.30	2.5	.91
Personal service workers	2.7	.94	2.6	.90	-.8	-.28	1.1	.37
Others	3.6	.47	3.4	.45	-.5	-.07	1.6	.21
Farmers	3.4	1.01	3.2	.95	2.5	.76	1.1	.34
Total	123.3	1.36	118.9	1.31	12.5	.14	53.1	.59

Because of the structure of the module, the industrial and regional patterns of labor demand are similar to the patterns of gross output; hence, they are not presented here.[10] Rather, the final results of the factor employment module—estimates of induced labor demand by *occupational* category—are presented.

Table 6.11 shows the effect of the net transfers from FAP and NIT on the demand for labor in several occupational categories. Simulations I and II show net increases in labor demand of 123,000 jobs for FAP and 119,000 jobs for NIT. The clerical workers and operatives categories experience the largest net increases—together they account for more than one-third of the national total in both simulations. The occupational impact indicators for these sectors are greater than the national indicator of 1.3.[11] Other occupational categories with impact indicators significantly higher than the national indicator are managers, officials, and proprietors (1.6–1.7) and sales workers (2.2). The occupations with the lowest indicators are professional and technical workers (1.0), service workers (.9), and farmers (1.0).

The other projections of labor demand for NIT in Simulations III and IV indicate smaller net increases in labor demand—only 13,000 and 53,000 jobs as opposed to the 119,000 jobs of Simulation II. The occupational patterns of these changes are also substantially different from those in Simulation II. The differences can best be seen by comparing the occupational impact indicators among the simulations. The general pattern of impact indicators relative to the national impact indicator of Simulation IV is similar to that of Simulation II, except for clerical workers.

The pattern of occupational demands of NIT Simulation III is substantially different from that of Simulations II and IV. The major occupational categories of professional, technical, and kindred workers and

---

[10] The industrial patterns for gross output and labor demands are not identical because labor–output ratios vary among production sectors. The regional patterns are not identical because the industrial composition of gross outputs varies among regions.

[11] The occupational impact indicator is the ratio of the program-induced employment in an occupation to .001 times the total employment in the occupation. Symbolically,

$$I_o^e = \frac{M_o}{.001\,(L_o)}$$

where I_o^e is the occupational impact indicator for occupation o, M_o is the program-induced change in labor demand in occupation o, and L_o is the total employment in occupation o in 1970.

service workers are estimated to experience absolute net *decreases* of demand. Only the operatives category is estimated to experience an increase of labor demand of more than 3000 jobs. In all of the occupational categories except farmers, the labor demand estimate of Simulation IV is intermediate to those of Simulations II and III.

Again, examination of the detailed categories suggests an explanation for the adverse effect of the programs on the employment of low-wage, low-skill workers relative to that of high-wage, high-skill workers.[12] In Simulation II (NIT), for example, the induced demand for a number of predominantly low-wage occupations is very small or negative, while that for some predominantly high-wage occupations is relatively large. Among the low-skill, low-wage occupations with very low induced demands are the following: textile operatives (with an impact indicator of −.18), personal service workers (.90), other service workers (.45), and farmers and farm workers (.95). Compare these impact indicators with the aggregate indicator of 1.31. While, according to Simulation II, these low-wage occupations confront an increased demand of about 9000 jobs (or 7.6 percent of the total of all induced labor demand), they have to experience an increase in demand of 19,500 jobs (or 16.4 percent of the total) if their share of total national employment is to remain constant from before to after the program.

Conversely, the demand increases for some predominantly high-skill, high-wage occupations yield impact indicators greater than the national indicator. For Simulation II, these include the major category of managers, officials, and proprietors (1.6) and the detailed categories of pharmacists (2.47), mining engineers (2.67), geologists and geophysicists (2.01), and ship officers, pilots, and bursars (2.32). The results for FAP (Simulation I) are similar to those for NIT. Again the conclusion is that the economic adjustments stimulated by income-transfer policy work to the advantage of relatively high-skill, high-wage workers and to the disadvantage of relatively low-skill, low-wage workers.

[12] Appendix L presents the labor demand impact indicators for the detailed occupational categories for both Simulation I (FAP) and Simulation II (NIT).

7

Summary and conclusions

The objective of this study is to extend the framework for analyzing the economic impacts of both existing and proposed income-transfer and taxation policies. We have pursued this objective by constructing an empirical simulation model designed to estimate the changes in consumption spending that would be brought about by a proposed policy and to trace the effects of these changes through the economy. We have estimated these effects in substantial detail, for regions, industries, occupations, and income classes. While the model and its empirical specification are not in themselves a complete evaluation framework, they do extend the available techniques for evaluating tax–transfer policies. In this final chapter, we summarize the major empirical results of the study and appraise some of its shortcomings as a comprehensive analysis of economic effects. In spite of its limitations, the study illuminates the policy implications of a number of issues; in the final section, a few of these implications are drawn.

A brief summary of empirical findings

In addition to estimating the impact of proposed income-support policies on detailed sectors of the economy, this study has uncovered a

125

number of more general allocative and distributional effects, that is, policy-induced shifts in incomes and economic activities among regions, occupational groups, and income classes.

The study documents the sizable flow to the South of net transfers from both FAP and NIT. The detailed regions designated as the South are predicted to receive 46 percent of gross transfers but to pay only about 26 percent of the taxes required to finance the programs. The South is estimated to receive over $650 million of *net* transfers under both FAP and NIT, implying an equivalent loss for the other regions of the country.

Although this pattern of net transfers tends to equalize the regional distribution of income, the study indicates that the pattern of production shifts resulting from these net transfers is substantially less equalizing. While consumption demands in the South stimulated by the policy increase retail purchases in southern states, a high proportion of the real production required by these purchases occurs outside the South. Much of this induced production occurs in the higher-income, more industrialized North Central states. As a consequence, treating the regional pattern of net transfers as indicative of the regional pattern of economic stimulation provided by the program is misleading. When the induced demands are traced through the economy, the South is seen to receive less economic stimulation than the patterns of direct net transfers and induced household expenditures imply. Conversely, the Northeast and North Central regions are relatively more favored than their shares of net transfers imply.

A similar disparity between direct and indirect effects is shown by the pattern of jobs created by the simulated policies. While the direct net transfers result in a shift of income from high-income to low-income families and a substantial equalization of the income distribution, the jobs created by the policy-induced demands tend to favor high-skill, high-wage occupations. Indeed, because of the policy, the relative structure of labor demands tends to shift away from low-wage, low-skill workers toward those with higher skills and earnings. Because of this pattern, the newly generated income is less equally distributed than total family income. Again, observing only the distribution pattern of the direct net transfers would yield an exaggerated picture of the equalizing effect of the policies.

As the empirical findings indicate, this adverse distribution of employment demands is a result of the consumption patterns of those who receive net transfers and those who pay more taxes to finance the programs. Low-income families, who in general gain from net transfers, tend to alter their consumption demands toward industries that are relatively heavy employers of high-wage, high-skill workers—motor vehicles, petroleum, and educational services. Conversely, the decreases in consumption by higher-income families tend to be concentrated on goods and services produced by lower-skill workers—textiles, apparel, and hotel services.

While this alteration in sectoral—industrial and occupational—patterns would occur even if no new income or employment were created by the policy, both NIT and FAP result in an expansion in aggregate demand in the economy. This expansion occurs in consumption spending (about $1.6 billion), gross output (about $3.0 billion), employment (about 120,000 jobs), and earnings (about $725 million). This expansionary impact results from the differences between the marginal propensities to spend of net beneficiaries of the program and those of net cost bearers. Because lower-income families have a higher marginal propensity to spend than the higher-income families who finance the transfer, an expansion in consumption is induced, and along with it an expansion in output, employment, and earnings. Like some of the other impacts, this expansionary effect is not immediately apparent from the direct effects of the policies.

Tracing the detailed patterns of policy-induced effects throughout the economy, then, reveals that the full impact of the policy on regions, industries, occupations, and income classes is different from that suggested by observing the direct effects alone. The indirect effects do not favor the poor or the South as much as the direct effects imply. Moreover, neither the expansion of industrial and labor demands nor the shift in their composition toward high-wage, high-skill sectors is suggested by the flows of direct transfers and taxes. Full evaluation of the policy requires consideration of both direct and indirect impacts.

Some caveats

The measures of program impact produced by the simulation model, while more comprehensive than earlier measures, nevertheless must be interpreted with some caution. As indicated earlier, our model is not a full general equilibrium model, and numerous important economic relationships are not included in its structure. Moreover, because of constraints imposed by available data, the resulting estimates are based on assumptions that, in all likelihood, deviate substantially from actual conditions in the economy. While we judge that our empirical results are roughly accurate portrayals of the size and composition of economic impacts, a brief catalog of the ways in which our approach falls short of the ideal framework is in order.

First, to facilitate the empirical development of the model, several behavioral responses to income-transfer policy have to be suppressed; no effects on induced labor supply, migration, or household structure are included in the model. Moreover, while the effects of transfer policy on consumption expenditures are estimated on the basis of both normal income and current income, our analysis of impacts covers only responses to changes in current disposable income. In estimating output and employment responses to these demand changes, Leontief production functions, implying homogeneity, linearity, and nonsubstitutability, are employed, and constant market prices are assumed. And, because of the short-run, current-account nature of the model, investment behavior induced by the policy—in particular, housing construction—is excluded. Because the model is not run recursively, adjustments in second, third, and *n*th periods are not estimated. Because of limitations in the data on household expenditures, induced changes in direct household employment—primarily the employment of domestic workers—are not recorded. Estimates of policy-induced changes in food and medical care expenditures are probably biased upward because of large increases in public subsidization of these purchases between the date of the consumption survey and the present. In estimating the pattern of induced occupational demands, constant earnings distributions within occupations and regions are assumed and one unverified assumption (out of many possible assumptions) is employed to distribute earnings increments among potential employees. Finally, no estimates are made of the distributional impacts of induced income streams other than earnings.

Although it cannot be verified empirically, it seems likely that relaxation of several of these assumptions would reinforce our general conclusion that the indirect effects of the policies work against the tendency of the direct impacts to favor the poor and the South. For example, policy-induced nonlabor income—rents, profits, interest, and so forth—would be expected to favor the rich more in its distribution than earned income. Hence, adding nonlabor income to the model would accentuate the tendency of indirect impacts to counteract direct impacts. Similarly, to the extent that induced effects on labor supply were admitted to the model, wage rates in the low-skill occupations would be expected to rise, causing employers to substitute capital and higher-skill labor for low-skill labor. Again, this would accentuate the shift in the demand for new employees away from relatively low-skill, low-wage workers. Finally, including induced demands for investment (for example, new housing) and household workers, or running the model recursively so as to include higher-order expenditure responses would likewise be expected to add to the relatively high-skill labor demands already identified.

Some policy implications

A number of policy implications flow from our numerical analyses. First, the regional and income redistributional impacts of direct tax–transfer schemes appear to be somewhat less powerful than estimates of their primary or direct incidence suggest. Given the pattern of indirect effects, transfer schemes with high first-round target efficiency may lose some of their edge when compared to, say, expenditure programs with high indirect impacts on the employment of low-skill workers.

Second, if the induced shift in the skill composition of labor demand is combined with the presumed reduction in the supply of low-skill labor, the second-, third-, and nth-year cost estimates of the transfer programs may well exceed the estimates of first-year cost presented here.

Third, for the public sector to effectively achieve a reduction in income poverty and an increase in the equality of the distribution of income, explicit policies to increase the demand for low-skill workers and perhaps to improve the quality of their jobs may be required.[1] This study has revealed the complexity of the processes by which any exogenous, demand-creating policy stimulates employment and earnings

---

[1] See, for example, U.S. Congress, Joint Economic Committee, *The American Distribution of Income: A Structural Problem,* by Lester C. Thurow and Robert E. B. Lucas, Joint Committee Print (Washington, D.C.: U.S. Government Printing Office, 1972) (Y4.Ec 7:In 2/7). The authors assert that "If a restructuring of incomes is desired, it can be brought about. Substantial efforts, however, must be directed toward altering the demand for labor as opposed to altering personal characteristics of individuals looking for work. Without such efforts on the demand side of the market, most programs for altering personal characteristics will have little payoff" (p. 46). For Thurow and Lucas, alterations in the demand for labor consist of both exogenous changes in labor demands by skill level and changes in the process by which labor demands become transformed into individual earnings.

For a discussion of the impact of the quality of low-wage jobs on the high unemployment rates of low-skill, primarily young, workers, see U.S. Congress, Joint Economic Committee, *Lowering the Permanent Rate of Unemployment,* by Martin S. Feldstein, Joint Committee Print (Washington, D.C.: U.S. Government Printing Office, 1973) (Y4.Ec 7:Un2/6).

among various occupations and regions. Given this complexity, any assertion that the public sector can or should design expenditure programs to promote employment and earnings increases for low-skill, low-wage workers must be approached with caution. The similarity of our estimates of the distribution of induced earnings with the distribution of total preprogram earned income testifies to the ability of the economic system to disperse the income generated by exogenous expenditures over the entire earnings and income distribution—and, perhaps, suggests why attempts to alter the inequality in the distribution of income in the United States have been so unsuccessful. Any proposal that relies on increases in the demand for labor but that leaves unaltered the processes by which changes in level of production influence individual earned incomes should be accompanied by detailed analyses of the sort provided by the model developed in this study. Given the existence of this model, we believe that the form of analysis presented here is now feasible for the entire gamut of expenditure proposals aimed at income redistribution. We urge that such analysis be undertaken by the appropriate public agencies.

Appendix A

Calculation of benefits from income-transfer programs

The benefits to households under the two transfer programs analyzed in this study were determined using the formulas displayed below.

Negative income tax (NIT)

For households with earned incomes, Y_e, of $720 or less per year, benefits, B, were calculated as

$$B = \text{Max} \left\{ 0, \left[G - .60(Y_u^1 + Y_u^2 + Y_u^3 + Y_u^4) \right] \right\}.$$

Benefits to households with earned incomes greater than $720 per year were determined by the formula

$$B = \text{Max} \left\{ 0, \left[G - .67(Y_e^1 - \$720) - .60(Y_u^1 + Y_u^2 + Y_u^3 + Y_u^4) \right] \right\}.$$

Family Assistance Plan (FAP)

For households with earned incomes of $720 or less per year,

$$B = \text{Max} \left\{ 0, \left[G - .67 \, Y_u^2 - Y_u^1 - Y_u^3 + P \right] \right\}.$$

For households with earned incomes of more than $720 per year, bene-
fits were determined by the formula

$$B = \text{Max} \left\{ 0, \left[G - .67 \left(Y_e^2 - \$720 + Y_u^2 \right) - Y_u^1 - Y_u^3 + P \right] \right\}.$$

where

G = the federal family income guarantee and is equal to $800 for
each of the first two persons in a family unit, plus $400 for each of the
next three persons, plus $300 for each of the next two persons, plus
$200 for any additional members of the family unit;

Y_e^1 = the sum of wages, salaries, incomes of children, self-employed
nonfarm income, and self-employed farm income;

Y_e^2 = Y_e^1 minus exempt children's incomes (which are defined as
children's incomes in excess of the sum of $2000 plus, if the family has
more than four members, $200 for each of the fifth through the ninth
family members);

Y_u^1 = the sum of the family's benefits from Aid to Families with
Dependent Children (AFDC) and Aid to Families with Dependent
Children-Unemployed Parent (AFDC-UP);

Y_u^2 = the amount of alimony payments;

Y_u^3 = the total of Social Security benefits, rental income, interest
receipts, dividends, pension income, Workmen's Compensation benefits, veterans' benefits, Unemployment Insurance benefits, private
transfer payments, and "other" income; and

P = the state supplementary welfare payment. (A detailed discussion of the calculation of state supplementary welfare payments is
presented in Appendix B.)

Appendix B

Simulated state supplementary welfare payments under FAP

For some families residing in states with relatively high Aid to Families with Dependent Children (AFDC) and Aid to Families with Dependent Children-Unemployed Parent (AFDC-UP) payment levels, the passage of the H.R. 1 form of the Family Assistance Plan (FAP) would entail a reduction in net income. This would occur because of the withdrawal of AFDC and AFDC-UP benefits simultaneously with the provision of Family Assistance benefits. It is likely that states would make supplementary payments to both existing beneficiaries and families eligible for public assistance before H.R. 1 in order to avoid having the legislative change make some families worse off. In the H.R. 1 bill, however, no provision is made either for mandatory payment of state supplementary benefits or for federal support to states should such benefits be paid. Nevertheless, in the H.R. 1 simulation, all states are assumed to adopt supplementary assistance programs for families eligible for federal assistance payments. The costs of the supplement are assumed to be shifted to the

This appendix was prepared with the assistance of John F. Moeller. Professor Moeller was a member of the Urban Institute staff that developed the microdata model for simulating the distribution of benefits from proposed income-transfer programs.

federal government. In this appendix, the procedures used to estimate the supplementary benefit payments and the assumptions on which they are based are presented. While the procedures and rules adopted are largely speculative, they seem to be in accord with what reasonable state behavior would be if H.R. 1 were enacted into law.

The first step in this simulation was to estimate which families were to be eligible for supplementary benefits. Current Population Survey (CPS) interview units[1] were accordingly processed by first omitting all aged and disabled adults. If the remaining family members satisfied any of the following requirements, a supplementary assistance payment was computed for the unit:

1. the family head was female and the unit contained related children[2];
2. the family head was male with no spouse present and the unit contained related children;
3. the male family head was disabled (an Aid to the Aged, Blind, and Disabled (ABD) categorically eligible person) but received no ABD payments, and his spouse was present in the unit along with their related children;
4. the family satisfied none of the above requirements yet resided in an AFDC-UP state, the male head was deemed unemployed and received no Unemployment Insurance, and the unit contained related children.[3]

In no instances were supplements imputed for intact families with children—the "working poor." Unrelated children living in the same household were grouped together and treated as a separate filing unit

---

[1]Subfamilies were *not* considered as separate interview units in this processing, but instead were merged into the interview unit containing the household head.

[2]Children were defined as any persons *not* satisfying any one of the following requirements defining an adult:

a. 22 years of age or older at survey time;
b. 18–21 years of age at survey time and *not* in school (current employment status listed as "in school," or worked zero weeks or 1–13 weeks during the base year because "in school");
c. 14–21 years of age and head or wife of head of a CPS interview unit (subfamilies were considered as separate interview units for this screen);
d. marital status on survey recorded as married, spouse present; married, spouse absent—in armed forces; married, spouse absent—other; or separated.

[3]States with AFDC-UP programs in June of 1970 were assumed to be the states supplementing FAP payments to UP families in 1973. Male heads were deemed unemployed if they were listed as part-time workers during the survey year or if they experienced any weeks of unemployment during the survey year.

for supplementary assistance payments.[4] The size of filing units for supplementary benefits was calculated by summing the number of children and adults assigned to the eligible units.

It should be noted that the microsimulation procedure used to compute the supplementary benefits applied a participation rate of 100 percent, that is, it assigned benefits to families eligible for but not actually receiving AFDC and AFDC-UP benefits. The relative gainers from enforcing full participation are eligible families in states with relatively high standards of need and relatively low participation rates. The participation rate for AFDC in 1973 was estimated to be over 95 percent, that for AFDC-UP only 12 percent.[5]

Computed supplementary assistance payments for eligible units were based on the following formula:

$$SUPP = min(MAXPAY, BUDEF);$$
$$BUDEF = max(O, COSTND - CHGINC);$$

where

SUPP = the computed supplementary payment;
MAXPAY = maximum payment level allowed for filing units of given sizes within the unit's state of residence;
COSTND = standard of need for categorical aid program varying by filing unit size; and
CHGINC = chargeable income or monetary resources of the filing unit offset against the cost standard in computing the unit's "budget deficit" (BUDEF).

State cost standards and maximum payment levels for supplementary benefits are those for AFDC and AFDC-UP units in June of 1970, adjusted to 1973 according to percentage changes in the Consumer Price Index. Figures for units with three and four members are published by the U.S. Department of Health, Education, and Welfare. Figures for units of other sizes were interpolated or extrapolated from these published numbers.

Alimony payments and earnings in excess of $720 per year were taxed at a 67 percent rate. Unearned income[6] (including federal bene-

---

[4]No federal Family Assistance Plan payments were computed for these filing units of unrelated children.

[5]See Harold Beebout, "Estimated AFDC Eligibility Under Alternative Accounting Period Assumptions" (internal memorandum, Mathematica, Inc., April, 1975).

[6]Unearned income in the CPS for family units eligible for supplementary payments consists of Social Security, Railroad Retirement, interest, rent, dividends, Unemployment Compensation, Workmen's Compensation, government employees' pensions, veterans' payments, private pensions, alimony, contributions, and "other" (a catchall category for miscellaneous income) sources of income.

fit payments) reduced supplementary benefits dollar for dollar. Earnings of children in school were excluded up to a maximum amount, which varied by size of filing unit (but in no case exceeded $3000 per year for any filing unit). Income of nonaged, nondisabled adults in the interview unit who were excluded from the filing unit count was treated as income available to the filing unit. All payments were computed on an annual basis.

If the head or the spouse of the head of an interview unit was aged or blind or disabled but was not eligible by income for adult aid, then this person's entire income was treated as available to any remaining filing unit in the interview unit. The income in excess of the state Old Age Assistance cost standard of any adult who was neither the head nor the head's spouse and who was eligible for but not receiving adult payments was lumped with that of a filing unit receiving federal family benefits in the same interview unit and taxed at 100 percent.

In these computations no special adjustments, justifiable under the "hold harmless" provision of H.R. 1, were made in state payment levels prior to computing the supplementary benefits. Since *reported* public assistance was included in the preprogram income of the filing units and *computed* federal payments and state supplementary benefits were included in a filing unit's postprogram income, there is no guarantee that simulated postprogram income will be greater than or equal to preprogram income for every interview unit.[7] However, since public assistance is underreported in the CPS (by about 20 percent in 1973), and since 100 percent participation is assumed for H.R. 1, the total net increase in disposable income generated in the simulation is likely to be biased upward to some unknown extent.

----

[7] Had eligibility rules for public assistance been simulated as they were for supplementary benefits, except for inclusion of taxable federal benefits, preprogram income would have been less than or equal to postprogram income for every unit.

Appendix C

Simulated tax revenues required to finance transfer programs

The simulation model designed to calculate the distribution of the costs of the program assumes that public expenditures for income transfers are financed by a surtax on the federal personal income tax. Because the programs entail varying net costs, the surtax rate varies from simulation to simulation. In this appendix, the rules used to simulate the income tax are described, as are some regional comparisons of the simulated taxes with actual tax payments.

The following assumptions are made in the tax simulations:

1. Taxpayers (filing units) are divided into two major groups:
    a. married—assumed to file jointly
    b. nonmarried—includes singles without dependents and unmarried household heads.
2. Total income is defined to *include* the following:
    a. wages and salaries
    b. dividends minus $200
    c. interest
    d. income from self-employment
    e. rental income

    f. pensions
    g. alimony
    h. contributions.

Total income is defined to *exclude* the following:
    a. Social Security
    b. disability payments
    c. unemployment benefits
    d. compensations
    e. veterans' benefits
    f. public assistance.

3. Taxable income is computed as follows:
   a. If total income is less than $10,000, the standard tax tables are employed, on the assumption that deductions are not itemized. Standard deductions and allowances for dependents are incorporated into these tables.
   b. If total income is more than $10,000, a "standard" deduction of the maximum of $650 or 15 percent of total income is subtracted from total income. Then $750 is multiplied by the number of exemptions and the product is subtracted from adjusted income. The net result is called taxable income. The tax liability is determined from Table I (for nonmarried filing units) and Table II (for married filing units) of the standard tax forms.

Estimates of income taxes by state and region for 1973 are shown in the following tables.

Table C.1 shows the simulated federal income taxes for 1973 aggregated by state together with actual 1973 tax yields reported by the Internal Revenue Service (IRS). Comparison of the two reveals that total simulated taxes by state are roughly equal to the reported yields. Discrepancies reflect sampling errors and errors in reporting income in the Current Population Survey (CPS) and the simplifications of the income tax rules embedded in the simulations. Total simulated tax yields were $95.975 billion compared with the IRS reported yields of $107.566 billion.

Table C.2 reports the same information aggregated to the 23 detailed regions and 4 census regions employed in the study. While there are some discrepancies in the percentage distributions between actual and estimated tax yields, the orders of magnitude are quite similar.

TABLE C.1

Simulated and actual federal income tax yields for 1973, by state (in millions of dollars)

State	Actual Income Tax after Credit [a]	Tax Simulations
Al	$ 1253	$ 1256
Az	984	878
Ar	666	445
Ca	11,024	11,809
Co	1297	1126
Ct	2189	1656
De	389	270
DC	454	419
Fl	4341	3497
Ga	2070	1781
Hi, Wy, Nv	1042	495
Il	7251	5874
In	2705	2357
Ia	1300	755
Ks	1113	866
Ky	1198	953
La	1357	1169
Me, Vt, NH	955	770
Md	2596	2709
Ma	3208	2550
Mi	5350	4463
Mn	1712	1726
Ms	621	619
Mo, ND, SD	2668	1798
Mt, Id, Ak	799	856
Nb	726	883
NJ	4854	4380
NM	390	228
NY	10,599	10,238
NC	2094	1726
Oh	5826	5563
Ok	1031	870
Or	1103	979
Pa	5954	5518
RI	476	478
SC	1005	1008
Tn	1724	1289
Tx	5621	4865
Ut	432	646
Va	2552	1976
Wa	1882	1504
WV	677	652
Wi	2078	2075
United States [b]	107,566	95,975

[a]The numbers in this column were drawn from U.S. Department of the Treasury, Internal Revenue Service, *Statistics of Income, Preliminary 1973: Individual Income Tax Returns*, publication 198(8–75) (Washington, D.C.: Department of the Treasury, 1975), Table 8, p. 28.

[b]Excluding APO/FPO, Puerto Rico, and Other.

TABLE C.2

Simulated and actual federal income tax yields, by region (in millions of dollars)

Region	1973 Actual		1973 Estimated	
	Income Tax after Credit	Percentage of Total Tax Yield	Tax Simulations	Percentage of Total Tax Yield
Northeast	$28,235	26.2	$25,590	26.7
Ct, Me, Ma, NH, RI, Vt	6828	6.3	5454	5.7
NY	10,599	9.9	10,238	10.7
Pa, NJ	10,808	10.0	9898	10.3
North Central	30,729	28.6	26,360	27.5
Oh, Mi	11,175	10.4	10,026	10.4
In, Il	9957	9.3	8231	8.6
Wi, Mn	3790	3.5	3801	3.9
Ia, Mo	3493	3.2	2295	2.4
Ks, Nb, ND, SD	2314	2.2	2007	2.1
South	29,649	27.6	25,504	26.6
De, DC, Md	3439	3.2	3398	3.5
Va, WV	3229	3.0	2628	2.7
NC	2094	2.0	1726	1.8
SC	1005	0.9	1008	1.1
Ga	2070	1.9	1781	1.9
Fl	4341	4.0	3497	3.6
Ky, Tn	2922	2.7	2242	2.3
Al	1253	1.2	1256	1.3
Ms	621	0.6	619	0.6
Ar, Ok	1697	1.6	1315	1.4
La	1357	1.3	1169	1.2
Tx	5621	5.2	4865	5.1
West	18,953	17.6	18,521	19.3
Az, Co, Id, NM, Ut, Nv, Wy, Mt, Ak	4451	4.1	3734	3.9
Wa, Or, Hi	3478	3.2	2978	3.1
Ca	11,024	10.3	11,809	12.3
United States	107,566 [a]		95,975	

[a] Excluding APO/FPO, Puerto Rico, and Other.

Appendix D

Estimation of marginal budget shares

The marginal budget shares used in Methods 1 and 2 of the consumption expenditure module were derived in the following manner.

A piecewise semi-log expenditure—income regression model

The specification of this expenditure system was chosen to capture the nonlinearities in relationships between consumption and income observed in previous studies. In this model, family expenditures on commodities and services in each of the 56 final demand categories were regressed against family income, family size, and several other non-income variables. In addition, all interaction terms between the income levels, age of head of household, regional variables, and tenure variables were included in each regression. The specific model for commodity k is as follows:

$$E^k = \beta_0{}^k + \beta_1{}^k X_1 + \beta_2{}^k X_2 + \cdots + \beta_{77}{}^k X_{77}, \tag{1}$$

where

E^k = family expenditure on commodity k;
$X_1 = \log D$ (D = family disposable income);
$X_2 = \max (0, \log D/a)$ (a = \$2000 in 1973 dollars);
$X_3 = \max (0, \log D/b)$ (b = \$3000 in 1973 dollars);
$X_4 = \max (0, \log D/c)$ (c = \$4000 in 1973 dollars);
$X_5 = \max (0, \log D/d)$ (d = \$5000 in 1973 dollars);
$X_6 = \max (0, \log D/e)$ (e = \$6000 in 1973 dollars);
$X_7 = \max (0, \log D/f)$ (f = \$12,000 in 1973 dollars);
$X_8 = \log$ (family size);
$X_9 = 1$ if age of head of household < 31, 0 otherwise;
$X_{10} = 1$ if age of head of household $\varepsilon [31, 45]$, 0 otherwise;
$X_{11} = 1$ if age of head of household > 64, 0 otherwise;
$X_{12} = 1$ if rural, 0 otherwise;
$X_{13} = 1$ if from Northeast, 0 otherwise;
$X_{14} = 1$ if from South, 0 otherwise;
$X_{15} = 1$ if from West, 0 otherwise;
$X_{16} = 1$ if head of household has college degree, 0 otherwise;
$X_{17} = 1$ if head of household has high school degree, 0 otherwise;
$X_{18} = 1$ if homeowner, 0 otherwise;
$X_{19} = 1$ if household is composed of husband and wife only, 0 otherwise;
$X_{20} = 1$ if household is composed of husband and wife, age of oldest child < 6, 0 otherwise;
$X_{21} = 1$ if household is composed of husband and wife, age of oldest child < 17, 0 otherwise;
$X_{22} = 1$ if household is composed of husband and wife, age of oldest child > 17, 0 otherwise;
$X_{23} = 1$ if other related or nonrelated persons besides children reside with husband and wife, 0 otherwise;
$X_{24} = 1$ if one-parent household, 0 otherwise;

variables $X_{25}, \ldots, X_{77}$ are the two-, three-, and four-way interactions between the seven disposable income variables, $X_1, \ldots, X_7$, and the non-income variables, X_{11}, X_{14}, and X_{18}; and

B_j^k = coefficients (to be estimated by OLS) ($j = 0, 1, \ldots 77$).

Observations with negative expenditures or negative incomes were removed from the sample.

The regressions were run using 1960–1961 expenditure data, and estimates of the income–expenditure β coefficients for each commodity were obtained. The data source for these regressions was the 1960–1961 Consumer Expenditure Survey of the U.S. Bureau of Labor Statistics.[1]

Calculation of commodity-specific estimates of marginal consumption propensity

By taking the first derivative of (1) with respect to disposable income, the marginal propensity to consume commodity k is obtained. Because of the nature of the income variable and because of the interaction terms, there are 56 marginal propensities for each commodity (7 income levels times 8 types of interaction). We can display these propensities in a 7 × 8 matrix, which we will call b^k. Denote the ith row of b^k as b_i^k and the jth column of b^k as b_j^k. In particular,

$$
\begin{aligned}
i = 1 &\rightarrow & D \leq a \\
i = 2 &\rightarrow & a \leq D \leq b \\
i = 3 &\rightarrow & b \leq D \leq c \\
i = 4 &\rightarrow & c \leq D \leq d \\
i = 5 &\rightarrow & d \leq D \leq e \\
i = 6 &\rightarrow & e \leq D \leq f \\
i = 7 &\rightarrow & f \leq D
\end{aligned}
$$

and

$j = 1$	head of household aged < 65, nonsoutherner, renter
$j = 2$	head of household aged ≥ 65, nonsoutherner, renter
$j = 3$	head of household aged < 65, southerner, renter
$j = 4$	head of household aged < 65, nonsoutherner, homeowner
$j = 5$	head of household aged ≥ 65, nonsoutherner, homeowner
$j = 6$	head of household aged ≥ 65, southerner, renter
$j = 7$	head of household aged < 65, southerner, homeowner
$j = 8$	head of household aged ≥ 65, southerner, homeowner.

---

[1]See U.S. Department of Labor, Bureau of Labor Statistics, *Consumer Expenditures and Income: Survey Guidelines*, Bulletin 1684, (Washington, D.C., 1971) (L2.3:1684), for a discussion of the statistical reliability of this survey.

For example,

$$
b_{4,4}{}^k = \frac{\partial E^k}{\partial D} \Bigg|
\begin{array}{l}
c \le D \le d \\
\text{head of household aged} \le 65 \\
\text{nonsoutherner} \\
\text{homeowner}
\end{array}
\qquad = \quad \frac{\displaystyle\sum_{i=1}^{4} \beta_i + \sum_{i=42}^{45} \beta_i}{D}. \tag{2}
$$

Midpoints of each income interval were used as proxies for D in the calculation of b^k. There was a total of 56 times 56, or 3136, marginal propensities in the expenditure system.

Adjustment of the marginal propensities of the lowest income class

The calculations just described yield extremely low estimates for the lowest income class, that is, the class with disposable income less than or equal to \$2000. This is because the data base could not distinguish between transitory and nontransitory current income. This biased downward the *marginal* propensities in that class.[2]

To adjust for this phenomenon, a weighted extrapolation was performed.

$$
\hat{b}_{1,j}{}^k = .71 \left(\frac{b_{2,j}{}^k + b_{3,j}{}^k + b_{4,j}{}^k}{3} \right) + .29 \left(\frac{b_{4,j}{}^k + b_{5,j}{}^k + b_{6,j}{}^k}{3} \right) \tag{3}
$$

for $j = 1, \ldots, 8$. And $b_1{}^k$ was replaced by $\hat{b}_1{}^k$.

Estimation of vectors of marginal budget shares

In order to transform the calculated (and adjusted) commodity-specific marginal propensities into commodity-specific marginal budget shares, the $b_{ij}{}^k$ were aggregated for each of the 56 cells.

$$
\sum_{k=1}^{56} b_{ij}{}^k, \qquad \text{for all } i = 1, \ldots, 7
$$
$$
\text{and } j = 1, \ldots, 8.
$$

[2] Persons temporarily in that income class would tend to be concentrated toward the lower end of the class and yet to have relatively high expenditures, so the slopes within that class would be small and, indeed, possibly negative.

TABLE D.1

Marginal propensities to consume for 56 cells (sum of commodity-specific marginal propensities)

	1	2	3	4	5	6	7	8
1	.89	1.00	1.11	.55	.89	.58	.81	.56
2	.80	1.15	.87	.72	1.09	.90	.75	.90
3	.78	.32	.61	.13	.40	.72	.67	.51
4	.91	1.28	1.51	.80	.92	.21	.84	.40
5	.40	.36	.13	.37	.08	1.02	.12	1.53
6	.76	.58	.69	.62	.60	.53	.68	.42
7	.52	.65	.68	.66	.68	.66	.66	.49

Note: The rows and columns of the matrices displayed in Tables D.1–D.4 correspond to the rows and columns of the matrix b^k described in section 2 of this appendix.

TABLE D.2

Marginal budget shares for expenditures on food and kindred products

	1	2	3	4	5	6	7	8
1	.26	.15	.20	.26	.16	.12	.18	.16
2	.33	.20	.31	.28	.26	.29	.13	.22
3	.23	.07	.05	.04	.36	.15	.25	.18
4	.20	.15	.21	.25	−.02	−.41	.16	.08
5	.05	.37	.74	.11	−.79	.14	.22	.31
6	.21	.26	.14	.20	.25	.21	.18	.15
7	.21	.26	.14	.18	.22	.49	.15	.13

TABLE D.3

Marginal budget shares for expenditures on motor vehicles

	1	2	3	4	5	6	7	8
1	.07	.01	.10	.07	.07	.06	.07	.03
2	−.06	.01	.05	.04	−.03	.03	.16	.08
3	.18	.29	.17	.28	.40	−.05	.00	−.10
4	.10	−.04	.09	.08	.04	.68	.07	.19
5	.28	.59	−.27	.31	.57	.25	.64	.17
6	.04	−.03	.09	.09	.11	.06	.09	−.03
7	.06	.02	.04	.04	.01	−.09	.04	.22

These numbers may be interpreted as the marginal propensities to consume out of current income for each of the 56 cells. They are displayed in Table D.1.

Then, each element in b^k was divided by the sum over k of the elements, to obtain the commodity-specific marginal budget shares.

$$\alpha_{ij}^k = \frac{b_{ij}^k}{\sum\limits_{k=1}^{56} b_{ij}^k} \quad \text{for} \quad i = 1, \ldots, 7 \quad \text{and} \quad j = 1, \ldots, 8.$$

It should be noted that

$$\sum_{k=1}^{56} \alpha_{ij}^k = 1 \quad \text{for} \quad i = 1, \ldots, 7 \quad \text{and} \quad j = 1, \ldots, 8.$$

Tables D.2 to D.4 display the marginal budget shares for three major final demand sectors—food and kindred products, motor vehicles, and finance and insurance.

TABLE D.4

Marginal budget shares for expenditures on finance and insurance

	1	2	3	4	5	6	7	8
1	−.01	.02	.01	.02	.04	.01	.07	.03
2	−.02	.02	.02	.01	.05	.07	.10	.01
3	.03	−.04	−.04	.19	−.02	−.02	.02	.13
4	−.02	.05	.04	.05	.06	−.07	.10	−.04
5	−.01	.02	−.44	.24	−.05	.08	.34	.05
6	.08	.02	.08	.10	.06	.02	.12	.07
7	.06	.03	.16	.12	.06	.03	.12	.07

Appendix E _____

Reconciliation of consumer expenditure categories with input—output categories

The reconciliation of consumer expenditure categories and input—output categories required for this study was based almost entirely on the reconciliation used by the Multiregional Input—Output Model (MRIO).[1]

However, use of the MRIO reconciliation required two modifications. The first modification was necessary because the Survey of Consumer Expenditures (SCE) data used in this project did not provide categories as detailed as the expenditure categories used in the MRIO study. However, several Bureau of Labor Statistics publications provide consumption data for the detailed categories used in the MRIO project.[2] Data from these publications were used to estimate approximate

_____

[1] Karen R. Polenske et al., "Appendix B: Alignment of 1960 Consumer Expenditures Survey Categories with the 80 Order Input—Output Industrial Classification," in *State Estimates of the Gross National Product, 1947, 1958, 1963*, by Karen R. Polenske et al. (Lexington, Mass.: Lexington Books, D.C. Heath, 1972), pp. 173–211.

[2] U.S. Department of Labor, Bureau of Labor Statistics, *Consumer Expenditures and Income; Detail of Expenditures and Income*, Supplement 3 to BLS Report no. 237-90 (USDA Report CES-12), Survey of Consumer Expenditures, 1960–61 (Washington, D.C.: U.S. Government Printing Office, 1966) (L2.71:237–90).

TABLE E.1
Alignment of consumer expenditure categories with input—output sectors

Consumption Category	Percentage Allocated to an Input–Output Sector	Input–Output Sectors
Food and alcoholic beverages	3.0	1. Livestock and products
	4.9	2. Other agricultural products
	.8	3. Forestry and fish products
	87.8	14. Food and kindred products
	.2	65. Transportation and warehousing
	.5	69. Wholesale and retail trade
	2.8	80. Imports
Tobacco	98.7	15. Tobacco manufacturing
	1.3	64. Miscellaneous manufacturing
Housing, total		
Shelter, total		
Rented dwelling	.7	7. Coal mining
	4.5	31. Petroleum, related industry
	6.0	68. Electricity, gas, water, and sanitation
	88.8	71. Real estate and rental
Owned dwelling, total		
Interest on mortgages and other expenses	100.0	70. Finance and insurance
Property insurance	100.0	70. Finance and insurance
Repairs and replacements	50.0	12. Maintenance and repair construction
	50.0	30. Paint and allied products
Owned vacation home, cabin, etc.	25.0	12. Maintenance and repair construction
	25.0	30. Paint and allied products
Lodging out of home city	95.0	72. Hotels, repair services except auto
	5.0	77. Medical and educational services, nonprofit organizations

148

Other real estate			71. Real estate and rental
Fuel, light, refrigeration and water, total		100.0	
Solid and petroleum fuels	NE	11.0	7. Coal mining
		1.8	20. Lumber and wood products
		87.2	31. Petroleum, related industry
	NC	21.0	7. Coal mining
		2.4	20. Lumber and wood products
		76.6	31. Petroleum, related industry
	S	27.5	7. Coal mining
		10.0	20. Lumber and wood products
		62.5	31. Petroleum, related industry
	W	9.4	7. Coal mining
		8.5	20. Lumber and wood products
		82.1	31. Petroleum, related industry
Gas and electricity		100.0	68. Electricity, gas, water, and sanitation
Water, sewage, garbage, and trash collection		93.5	68. Electricity, gas, water, and sanitation
		6.5	79. State and local government enterprises
Ice, water softening services, freezer rentals, etc.		33.0	14. Food and kindred products
		33.0	65. Transportation and warehousing
		34.0	73. Business services
Household operations, total		100.0	66. Communications, except broadcasting
Telephone and telegraph		40.0	72. Hotels, repair services except auto
Other household services		20.0	65. Transportation and warehousing
less than $15,000		20.0	86. Household industry
		66.0	86. Household industry
$15,000 or more		34.0	72. Hotels, repair services except auto
		2.2	14. Food and kindred products
Household supplies		20.7	24. Paper and allied products
		1.2	25. Paperboard containers

(Continued)

149

TABLE E.1 continued

Consumption Category	Percentage Allocated to an Input–Output Sector	Input–Output Sectors
	7.2	26. Printing and publishing
	5.9	27. Chemicals, selected products
	1.4	28. Plastics and synthetics
	49.1	29. Drugs and cosmetics
	1.4	36. Stone and clay products
	2.3	38. Primary nonferrous metals manufacturing
	8.6	78. Federal government enterprises
House furnishings and equipment, total		
Household textiles	31.0	16. Fabrics
	1.0	17. Textile products
	64.0	19. Miscellaneous textile products
	1.0	32. Rubber, miscellaneous plastics
	2.0	54. Household appliances
Furniture, total	98.0	22. Household furniture
	2.0	83. Scrap and used goods
Floor coverings	75.0	17. Textile products
	25.0	64. Miscellaneous manufacturing
Major appliances, total	100.0	54. Household appliances
Small appliances	100.0	54. Household appliances
Housewares, total	10.0	19. Miscellaneous textile products
	4.0	20. Lumber and wood products
	14.0	32. Rubber, miscellaneous plastics
	11.0	35. Glass and glass products
	10.0	36. Stone and clay products
	17.0	41. Screw machine products, etc.
	8.0	42. Other fabricated metal products
	21.0	64. Miscellaneous manufacturing
	6.0	80. Imports

Category		
Insurance on furnishings, equipment, and apparel	100.0	
Other	4.5	70. Finance and insurance
	7.0	20. Lumber and wood products
	6.0	23. Other furniture
	7.0	34. Footwear, leather products
	13.2	36. Stone and clay products
	19.4	42. Other fabricated metal products
	7.0	44. Farm machinery, equipment
	23.3	51. Office, computing machines
	5.0	55. Electric lighting equipment
	8.0	62. Professional and scientific instruments
		64. Miscellaneous manufacturing
Clothing, clothing materials, and clothing services, total		
Clothing, total	94.0	18. Apparel
	3.0	34. Footwear, leather products
	2.0	80. Imports
Footwear, total	10.0	32. Rubber, miscellaneous plastics
	88.0	34. Footwear, leather products
	2.0	80. Imports
Jewelry and watches, total	3.0	34. Footwear, leather products
	14.3	62. Professional and scientific instruments
	79.0	64. Miscellaneous manufacturing
	2.2	80. Imports
	1.5	83. Scrap and used goods
Clothing materials	100.0	16. Fabrics
Clothing upkeep	100.0	72. Hotels, repair services except auto
Transportation, total		
Automobile purchase	89.0	59. Motor vehicles, equipment
	11.0	83. Scrap and used goods

(Continued)

TABLE E.1 continued

Consumption Category	Percentage Allocated to an Input–Output Sector	Input–Output Sectors
Automobile operation		
Gasoline, motor oil	100.0	31. Petroleum, related industry
Other auto operation	21.0	32. Rubber, miscellaneous plastics
	4.0	58. Miscellaneous electric machinery
	3.0	59. Motor vehicles, equipment
	67.0	75. Auto repair service
	4.0	76. Amusements
Public transportation, car pools, other	50.0	65. Transportation and warehousing
	3.0	31. Petroleum, related industry
	5.0	43. Engines and turbines
	31.0	61. Other transportation equipment
Medical care, total		
Prepaid care (premiums)	11.0	70. Finance and insurance
	89.0	77. Medical and educational services, nonprofit organizations
Services		
Direct expenses, total	100.0	77. Medical and educational services, nonprofit organizations
Eye care, including glasses	100.0	63. Optical, photographic equipment
Drugs and medicines	100.0	29. Drugs and cosmetics
Medical appliances, supplies, other	8.0	32. Rubber, miscellaneous plastics
	24.0	62. Professional and scientific instruments
Personal care, total		
Services	100.0	72. Hotels, repair services except auto
Supplies	14.0	24. Paper and allied products
	73.0	29. Drugs and cosmetics
	6.0	42. Other fabricated metal products
	3.0	54. Household appliances
	4.0	64. Miscellaneous manufacturing

Recreation, total		
Television and radio, phonographs, musical instruments, etc.	65.0	56. Radio, TV, etc. equipment
	8.0	57. Electronic components
	6.0	64. Miscellaneous manufacturing
	20.0	72. Hotels, repair services except auto
	100.0	76. Amusements
Spectator admissions		
Participant sports (equipment, fees, dues) and club dues, hobbies, pets, toys, recreation out of home city, other	7.0	13. Ordnance and accessories
	16.0	63. Medical, photographic equipment
	36.0	64. Miscellaneous manufacturing
	21.0	76. Amusements
	18.0	77. Medical and educational services, nonprofit organizations
Reading	100.0	26. Printing and publishing
Education		
Tuition and fees and music and other special lessons	100.0	77. Medical and educational services, nonprofit organizations
School books, supplies, equipment	69.0	26. Printing and publishing
	31.0	64. Miscellaneous manufacturing
Miscellaneous personal consumption expenditures (.3 of this category has been allocated as follows)	32.0	14. Food and kindred products
	38.0	72. Hotels, repair services except auto
	24.0	65. Transportation and warehousing
	6.0	76. Amusements

(Continued)

153

TABLE E.1 contuned

Consumption Category	Percentage Allocated to an Input–Output Sector	Input–Output Sectors
Personal insurance, total, nongovernmental	100.0	70. Finance and insurance
Gifts and contributions, total (cash, goods, services)		
To persons not in family (.67 of this category has been allocated as follows)		
	4.0	2. Other agricultural products
	64.0	14. Food and kindred products
	16.0	18. Apparel
	4.0	26. Printing and publishing
	5.0	29. Drugs and cosmetics
	4.0	54. Household appliances
	4.0	64. Miscellaneous manufacturing
To organizations	100.0	77. Medical and educational services, nonprofit organizations
Value of home-produced food		
	31.0	1. Livestock and products
	28.0	2. Other agricultural products
	41.0	14. Food and kindred products

breakdowns of the broader SCE categories presented on the tape used in this study. These breakdowns could then be related directly to the MRIO reconciliation categories.

The other modification of the MRIO reconciliation resulted from the extensive detail employed in the MRIO in attributing consumption categories to input–output industry categories. In some minor expenditure categories, some extremely small percentages were allocated to separate industries. To avoid excessive programming and computational effort, these minute allocations were eliminated, and the remaining allocations were rounded upward to absorb these small quantities.

Table E.1 contains a list of the consumer expenditure categories and the percentage allocations of each expenditure category to the various input–output categories, as used in this project.

Appendix F

The formation of socioeconomic groups for expenditure models based on normal income

In estimating the responses of consumption expenditures to a change in income-transfer policy, two empirical approaches are adopted in the study. The first is based on current income, the second on normal income. To implement the latter approach, households are first grouped by permanent socioeconomic characteristics. Next, the mean income transfer received by households in the socioeconomic group to which a household belongs is taken to be that household's expected transfer.

In moving from the estimation of expected transfer based on normal income to the estimation of induced consumption expenditures, two approaches are followed. As described in Chapter 4, one of these approaches is based on average budget shares, the other on marginal budget shares. Both approaches base estimates of family consumption responses on characteristics of the normal-income group to which the family belongs. In the approach based on normal income and average budget shares, induced household consumption patterns are estimated by first allocating the program-induced increments to disposable income to consumption expenditures and savings in the same ratio as total income is so allocated in the group to which the household belongs. Next, the increment to consumption expenditures is allocated among commodities as total consumption expenditures of the group were allocated prior to the policy change. In the approach based on normal income and marginal budget shares, estimated marginal propensities to spend and marginal budget shares conforming to the mean income of the group to which a family belongs are used to determine the family's induced expenditures and their allocation among commodity classes.

In this appendix, the composition of these socioeconomic groups is described and some of their economic characteristics are presented.

The data

In estimating consumption expenditures by the approach based on normal income, homogeneous groups had to be developed for both the survey data employed in estimating transfer payments and the survey data containing detailed commodity-consumption characteristics. The former body of data was the RIM tape, based on the 1971 Current Population Survey, the Census Bureau's annual sample survey of approximately 50,000 families. The latter data base was the 1960–1961 Bureau of Labor Statistics Survey of Consumer Expenditures. This data base contains records for 13,728 consumer units. Each record contains detailed classifications of sources of income, changes in assets, and types of expenditure by detailed commodity classification. Certain types of household units were deleted, including units headed by members of the armed forces and units whose head was working for pay but with no reported occupation. In addition, records with confusing or contradictory data relating to earned income, work status, or family-head status were dropped. The records remaining after this winnowing numbered 12,426.

Grouping the observations

The consumer units were placed into 177 groups in the following manner, depending on whether or not the head of the unit was working for pay at the time of the survey.

1. *Head working for pay (142 groups).* The consumption units in occupational groups 1–8 were assigned to group J_{abc}, where the subscripts refer to the following:

a. Occupation (eight possible values):
1. professional, technical, and kindred
2. managers, officials, and proprietors (nonfarm)
3. farmers and farm managers
4. clerical and kindred workers
5. sales
6. skilled
7. semiskilled
8. unskilled
9. not working, retired
10. not working, not retired
b. Age (four possible values):
1. 0–29 years
2. 30–44 years
3. 45–64 years
4. 65 and older
c. Family size (five possible values):
1. one person
2. two persons
3. three persons
4. four persons
5. five or more persons

2. *Head not working for pay (35 groups).* The consumption units in occupational groups 9 and 10 were assigned to group J'_{def}, where subscripts refer to the following:

d. Age (four possible values; same as b)
e. Family size (five possible values; same as c)
f. After-tax income group (three possible values). The grouping levels for subscript f depend on the specific values assumed by d and e. The income classes for a given d and e were specified so that each group J'_{def} contained a reasonable number of observations.

The total number of socioeconomic groups in J and J' was 177.

The socioeconomic groups and their economic characteristics

In Table F.1, data on the 177 socioeconomic groups are displayed, including data on the number of households in the nation in each group (derived from weights applied to sample survey observations), the mean income of each group, the transfers per household received by each group from the negative income tax plan, and the cell average propensity to consume.

TABLE F.1
177 socioeconomic groups and selected characteristics

Group (characteristic codes)	Number of Households (in thousands)	Mean Family Income	Mean Gross Transfers from Negative Income Tax	Cell Average Propensity to Consume
1 (F.S.1, A 1, Oc. 1)	738	$ 7,933	$ 0	1.06
2 (F.S.2, A 1, Oc. 1)	534	14,632	4	.97
3 (F.S.3, A 1, Oc. 1)	385	13,192	27	1.04
4 (F.S.4, A 1, Oc. 1)	253	14,278	0	.98
5 (F.S.5, A 1, Oc. 1)	105	13,738	35	1.09
6 (F.S.1, A 2, Oc. 1)	433	12,186	0	1.02
7 (F.S.2, A 2, Oc. 1)	265	19,850	0	.81
8 (F.S.3, A 2, Oc. 1)	351	18,023	23	1.02
9 (F.S.4, A 2, Oc. 1)	746	19,144	6	.93
10 (F.S.5, A 2, Oc. 1)	1,135	20,460	13	.96
11 (F.S.1, A 3, Oc. 1)	513	12,061	0	.91
12 (F.S.2, A 3, Oc. 1)	770	21,103	0	.82
13 (F.S.3, A 3, Oc. 1)	433	22,916	16	.94
14 (F.S.4, A 3, Oc. 1)	385	24,541	29	.88
15 (F.S.5, A 3, Oc. 1)	490	26,106	3	.93
16 (F.S.1, A 4, Oc. 1)	149	7,868	0	.85
17 (F.S.2, A 4, Oc. 1)	200	17,136	0	.88
18 (F.S.3–5, A 4, Oc. 1)	40	20,503	0	.82
19 (F.S.1, A 1, Oc. 2)	209	9,794	0	.92
20 (F.S.2, A 1, Oc. 2)	243	14,070	0	1.09
21 (F.S.3, A 1, Oc. 2)	210	12,972	35	1.08
22 (F.S.4, A 1, Oc. 2)	196	13,257	31	.83
23 (F.S.5, A 1, Oc. 2)	109	15,996	75	.93
24 (F.S.1, A 2, Oc. 2)	208	12,533	0	.97
25 (F.S.2, A 2, Oc. 2)	213	16,798	8	.91

26 (F.S.3, A 2, Oc. 2)	325	17,311	33	.96
27 (F.S.4, A 2, Oc. 2)	679	18,263	12	.91
28 (F.S.5, A 2, Oc. 2)	1,240	19,154	48	.99
29 (F.S.1, A 3, Oc. 2)	293	13,319	0	.99
30 (F.S.2, A 3, Oc. 2)	1,221	18,554	0	.88
31 (F.S.3, A 3, Oc. 2)	756	22,049	14	.83
32 (F.S.4, A 3, Oc. 2)	623	22,976	31	.93
33 (F.S.5, A 3, Oc. 2)	634	23,199	24	.89
34 (F.S.1, A 4, Oc. 2)	87	11,068	0	.83
35 (F.S.2, A 4, Oc. 2)	317	15,142	0	.78
36 (F.S.3–5, A 4, Oc. 2)	97	18,384	14	.66
37 (F.S.1–2, A 1, Oc. 3)	24	7,350	0	1.05
38 (F.S.3, A 1, Oc. 3)	24	5,648	649	1.05
39 (F.S.4, A 1, Oc. 3)	36	6,336	418	.67
40 (F.S.5, A 1, Oc. 3)	16	7,844	586	.73
41 (F.S.1–2, A 2, Oc. 3)	30	7,243	0	.59
42 (F.S.3, A 2, Oc. 3)	41	8,564	263	.69
43 (F.S.4, A 2, Oc. 3)	67	10,518	279	.79
44 (F.S.5, A 2, Oc. 3)	201	9,249	557	.76
45 (F.S.1, A 3, Oc. 3)	43	4,047	0	.93
46 (F.S.2, A 3, Oc. 3)	280	7,231	6	.69
47 (F.S.3, A 3, Oc. 3)	191	7,875	129	.79
48 (F.S.4, A 3, Oc. 3)	121	9,550	222	.84
49 (F.S.5, A 3, Oc. 3)	160	10,939	467	.75
50 (F.S.1, A 4, Oc. 3)	79	4,261	0	.88
51 (F.S.2, A 4, Oc. 3)	202	8,757	0	.74
52 (F.S.3, A 4, Oc. 3)	49	9,313	4	.73
53 (F.S.4, A 4, Oc. 3)	14	10,277	0	.86
54 (F.S.5, A 4, Oc. 3)	7	10,954	0	.61
55 (F.S.2, A 1, Oc. 4)	301	10,158	49	1.05
56 (F.S.3, A 1, Oc. 4)	272	10,911	67	1.05
57 (F.S.4, A 1, Oc. 4)	154	11,254	42	1.12

(Continued)

TABLE F.1 continued

162

Group (characteristic codes)	Number of Households (in thousands)	Mean Family Income	Mean Gross Transfers from Negative Income Tax	Cell Average Propensity to Consume
58 (F.S.5, A 1, Oc. 4)	64	9,819	182	1.01
59 (F.S.1, A 2, Oc. 4)	251	8,041	0	1.07
60 (F.S.2, A 2, Oc. 4)	214	12,277	16	.90
61 (F.S.3, A 2, Oc. 4)	253	11,459	58	1.04
62 (F.S.4, A 2, Oc. 4)	273	13,345	52	1.00
63 (F.S.5, A 2, Oc. 4)	378	14,660	24	.98
64 (F.S.1, A 3, Oc. 4)	688	8,021	0	.91
65 (F.S.2, A 3, Oc. 4)	652	13,117	4	.95
66 (F.S.3, A 3, Oc. 4)	318	16,748	3	.98
67 (F.S.4, A 3, Oc. 4)	223	18,057	36	1.04
68 (F.S.5, A 3, Oc. 4)	198	18,850	16	1.00
69 (F.S.1, A 4, Oc. 4)	183	6,523	0	.90
70 (F.S.2, A 4, Oc. 4)	114	10,293	0	.81
71 (F.S.1, A 1, Oc. 4–5)	835	5,767	0	1.04
72 (F.S.3–5, A 4, Oc. 4–5)	77	16,621	0	.91
73 (F.S.2, A 1, Oc. 5)	157	12,823	26	1.02
74 (F.S.3, A 1, Oc. 5)	164	12,202	29	1.10
75 (F.S.4, A 1, Oc. 5)	111	12,867	146	1.08
76 (F.S.5, A 1, Oc. 5)	40	12,746	142	1.19
77 (F.S.1, A 2, Oc. 5)	61	12,635	0	1.11
78 (F.S.2, A 2, Oc. 5)	96	13,665	33	1.04
79 (F.S.3, A 2, Oc. 5)	148	15,817	4	1.05
80 (F.S.4, A 2, Oc. 5)	243	16,931	28	1.04
81 (F.S.5, A 2, Oc. 5)	371	17,781	30	1.09
82 (F.S.1, A 3, Oc. 5)	167	5,910	0	1.20
83 (F.S.2, A 3, Oc. 5)	431	16,184	6	.92
84 (F.S.3, A 3, Oc. 5)	219	18,001	0	1.00
85 (F.S.4, A 3, Oc. 5)	199	20,996	23	1.02

86 (F.S.5, A 3, Oc. 5)	151	21,087	10	1.05
87 (F.S.1, A 4, Oc. 5)	71	7,100	0	1.00
88 (F.S.2, A 4, Oc. 5)	165	11,590	0	.93
89 (F.S.1, A 1, Oc. 6)	165	6,563	0	1.10
90 (F.S.2, A 1, Oc. 6)	445	12,083	13	1.01
91 (F.S.3, A 1, Oc. 6)	525	12,284	14	1.07
92 (F.S.4, A 1, Oc. 6)	459	12,250	13	1.14
93 (F.S.5, A 1, Oc. 6)	250	12,173	49	1.12
94 (F.S.1, A 2, Oc. 6)	179	10,321	0	1.04
95 (F.S.2, A 2, Oc. 6)	257	14,569	0	.83
96 (F.S.3, A 2, Oc. 6)	478	13,671	13	.96
97 (F.S.4, A 2, Oc. 6)	817	14,368	13	.97
98 (F.S.5, A 2, Oc. 6)	1,617	14,056	46	.97
99 (F.S.1, A 3, Oc. 6)	274	8,160	0	.90
100 (F.S.2, A 3, Oc. 6)	1,435	13,652	2	.80
101 (F.S.3, A 3, Oc. 6)	921	15,943	8	.93
102 (F.S.4, A 3, Oc. 6)	673	17,290	10	.95
103 (F.S.5, A 3, Oc. 6)	729	16,719	24	.94
104 (F.S.1, A 4, Oc. 6)	45	5,136	0	.94
105 (F.S.2, A 4, Oc. 6)	238	10,000	0	.79
106 (F.S.3–5, A 4, Oc. 6)	64	15,919	3	.82
107 (F.S.1, A 1, Oc. 7)	328	5,204	0	1.02
108 (F.S.2, A 1, Oc. 7)	488	9,975	27	1.05
109 (F.S.3, A 1, Oc. 7)	605	9,893	26	1.06
110 (F.S.4, A 1, Oc. 7)	509	9,959	73	1.04
111 (F.S.5, A 1, Oc. 7)	334	10,196	98	1.07
112 (F.S.1, A 2, Oc. 7)	243	7,057	0	.95
113 (F.S.2, A 2, Oc. 7)	294	10,614	29	.90
114 (F.S.3, A 2, Oc. 7)	435	11,359	19	.92
115 (F.S.4, A 2, Oc. 7)	639	12,881	23	1.03
116 (F.S.5, A 2, Oc. 7)	1,386	12,368	67	1.02
117 (F.S.1, A 3, Oc. 7)	537	6,830	0	.98
118 (F.S.2, A 3, Oc. 7)	1,190	11,541	2	.89
119 (F.S.3, A 3, Oc. 7)	697	13,362	9	.91
120 (F.S.4, A 3, Oc. 7)	516	14,866	10	.98

(Continued)

TABLE F.1 continued

Group (characteristic codes)	Number of Households (in thousands)	Mean Family Income	Mean Gross Transfers from Negative Income Tax	Cell Average Propensity to Consume
121 (F.S.5, A 3, Oc. 7)	605	14,943	53	1.01
122 (F.S.1, A 4, Oc. 7)	93	5,125	0	.98
123 (F.S.2, A 4, Oc. 7)	164	8,170	0	.84
124 (F.S.3–5, A 4, Oc. 7)	43	14,759	0	.86
125 (F.S.1, A 1, Oc. 8)	564	3,509	0	1.34
126 (F.S.2, A 1, Oc. 8)	443	8,914	104	1.08
127 (F.S.3, A 1, Oc. 8)	386	8,554	130	1.11
128 (F.S.4, A 1, Oc. 8)	265	9,105	103	1.15
129 (F.S.5, A 1, Oc. 8)	199	8,477	379	1.06
130 (F.S.1, A 2, Oc. 8)	336	5,680	0	1.09
131 (F.S.2, A 2, Oc. 8)	218	8,337	94	1.01
132 (F.S.3, A 2, Oc. 8)	276	9,260	169	1.16
133 (F.S.4, A 2, Oc. 8)	462	10,350	125	1.06
134 (F.S.5, A 2, Oc. 8)	940	10,774	254	1.09
135 (F.S.1, A 3, Oc. 8)	927	4,613	0	1.06
136 (F.S.2, A 3, Oc. 8)	1,106	9,775	21	.93
137 (F.S.3, A 3, Oc. 8)	622	11,762	59	.93
138 (F.S.4, A 3, Oc. 8)	404	13,042	73	.96
139 (F.S.5, A 3, Oc. 8)	638	13,628	131	1.02
140 (F.S.1, A 4, Oc. 8)	324	3,846	0	.89
141 (F.S.2, A 4, Oc. 8)	400	7,565	1	.81
142 (F.S.3–5, A 4, Oc. 8)	159	12,063	52	.78
143 (F.S.1, A 3, Inc.1–3, Oc. 9)	45	1,225	0	1.34
144 (F.S.1, A 3, Inc.4–9, Oc. 9)	91	7,338	0	.90
145 (F.S.2, A 3, Inc.1–3, Oc. 9)	13	929	0	1.29
146 (F.S.2, A 3, Inc.4–6, Oc. 9)	49	2,793	0	.93

147 (F.S.2, A 3, Inc.7–9, Oc. 9)	157	10,422	0	.88
148 (F.S.3, A 3, Inc.1–6, Oc. 9)	10	1,893	887	1.05
149 (F.S.3, A 3, Inc.7–9, Oc. 9)	39	11,248	0	.86
150 (F.S.4–5, A 3, Inc.1–8, Oc. 9)	7	3,208	402	.94
151 (F.S.4–5, A 3, Inc.9, Oc. 9)	30	14,048	0	.67
152 (F.S.1, A 4, Inc.1–3, Oc. 9)	2,058	1,377	0	1.16
153 (F.S.1, A 4, Inc.4–5, Oc. 9)	1,393	2,428	0	.98
154 (F.S.1, A 4, Inc.6–7, Oc. 9)	808	3,729	0	.82
155 (F.S.1, A 4, Inc.8–9, Oc. 9)	478	9,163	0	.77
156 (F.S.2, A 4, Inc. 1–3, Oc. 9)	329	1,197	31	1.10
157 (F.S.2, A 4, Inc.4–5, Oc. 9)	568	2,522	0	.96
158 (F.S.2, A 4, Inc.6–7, Oc. 9)	1,160	3,982	0	.82
159 (F.S.2, A 4, Inc.8–9, Oc. 9)	1,790	9,281	0	.71
160 (F.S.3, A 4, Inc.1–5, Oc. 9)	56	2,114	373	.95
161 (F.S.3, A 4, Inc.6–8, Oc. 9)	105	4,394	2	.93
162 (F.S.3, A 4, Inc.9, Oc. 9)	352	13,922	0	.75
163 (F.S.4–5, A 4, Inc.1–5, Oc. 9)	24	1,955	1,283	1.15
164 (F.S.4–5, A 4, Inc.6–8, Oc. 9)	71	4,374	313	.90
165 (F.S.4–5, A 4, Inc.9, Oc. 9)	205	14,856	0	.95
166 (F.S.1–2, A 1–2, Inc.1–3, Oc. 10)	452	429	233	1.01
167 (F.S.1–2, A 1–2, Inc.4–9, Oc. 10)	240	3,759	116	.91
168 (F.S.3–4, A 1–2, Inc.1–3, Oc. 10)	165	22	1,981	1.19
169 (F.S.3–4, A 1–2, Inc.4–9, Oc. 10)	430	4,431	435	.84
170 (F.S.5, A 1–2, Inc.1–5, Oc. 10)	139	886	2,533	1.32
171 (F.S.5, A 1–2, Inc.6–9, Oc. 10)	304	5,718	574	1.01
172 (F.S.1, A 3, Inc.1, Oc. 10)	210	211	0	1.20
173 (F.S.1, A 3, Inc.2–9, Oc. 10)	636	2,724	0	.84
174 (F.S.2, A 3, Inc.1–2, Oc. 10)	95	−733	232	1.17
175 (F.S.2, A 3, Inc.3–9, Oc. 10)	386	4,208	40	1.01
176 (F.S.3–5, A 3, Inc.1–4, Oc. 10)	115	262	1,498	1.09
177 (F.S.3–5, A 3, Inc.5–9, Oc. 10)	321	5,726	304	.94
Total	66,089			

Appendix G

Estimation of ratios of employment to output, by industry and region

The matrix of ratios of employment to output used to transform the sectoral gross outputs into employment demands in the factor employment module was constructed from data reported in the MRIO study.[1] In that study, sectoral gross output and employment aggregates, derived from the national input–output study and the Census of Manufactures, were presented for the years 1947, 1958, and 1963. Compound productivity growth rates were assumed. To project the ratios of employment to output for each of the 1817 regional industries to 1973, the rate of exponential decrease of these ratios was calculated and extrapolated forward to 1973.

The projection for each regional industry involved two steps.

Step 1:
$$r = \left[\frac{\sigma_{1963}}{\sigma_{1947}} \right]^{1/16} - 1.$$

[1] The MRIO model is described in Karen R. Polenske, *The United States Multiregional Input–Output Model* (Lexington, Mass.: Lexington Books, D.C. Heath, forthcoming).

Step 2: $\hat{\sigma}_{1973} = \sigma_{1963} (1 + r)^{10}$, where

r = rate of exponential decrease of σ;

σ_i = ratio of employment to output, $i = 1947, 1963$; and

$\hat{\sigma}_{1973}$ = projected 1973 ratio of employment to output.

TABLE G.1

**Average rates of coefficient change and
1973 ratios of employment to output, by industry**

Industry	r	$\hat{\sigma}_{1973}$
1 Livestock and products*	−.0276	.0211
2 Other agricultural products*	−.0333	.0279
3 Forestry and fishery products*	−.0354	.0467
4 Agriculture, forestry, and fishery services	.0000	.0974
5 Iron and ferroalloy ores mining*	−.0206	.0243
6 Nonferrous metal ores mining*	−.0635	.0203
7 Coal mining*	−.0622	.0290
8 Crude petroleum, natural gas*	−.0309	.0107
9 Stone and clay mining*	−.0378	.0386
10 Chemical and fertilizer mineral mining*	−.0274	.0255
11 New construction	−.0209	.0303
12 Maintenance and repair construction	−.0154	.0339
13 Ordnance and accessories*	−.1009	.0180
14 Food and kindred products*	−.0226	.0182
15 Tobacco manufactures*	−.0329	.0075
16 Fabrics*	−.0398	.0288
17 Textile products*	−.0489	.0209
18 Apparel*	−.0261	.0580
19 Miscellaneous textile products*	−.0537	.0342
20 Lumber and wood products*	−.0376	.0380
21 Wooden containers*	−.0169	.0689
22 Household furniture*	−.0204	.0554
23 Other furniture*	−.0055	.0563
24 Paper and allied products*	−.0271	.0253
25 Paperboard containers*	−.0264	.0335
26 Printing and publishing*	−.0060	.0535
27 Chemicals, selected products*	−.0496	.0146
28 Plastics and synthetics*	−.0665	.0132
29 Drugs and cosmetics*	−.0575	.0121
30 Paints and allied products*	−.0176	.0217
31 Petroleum, related industry*	−.0517	.0044
32 Rubber, miscellaneous plastics*	−.0276	.0344
33 Leather tanning, products*	−.0186	.0316
34 Footwear, leather products*	−.0093	.0797
35 Glass and glass products*	−.0198	.0430
36 Stone and clay products*	−.0262	.0357

TABLE G.1 continued

Industry	r	$\hat{\sigma}_{1973}$
37 Primary iron, steel manufacturing*	−.0218	.0282
38 Primary nonferrous metals manufacturing*	−.0077	.0232
39 Metal containers*	−.0212	.0217
40 Heating, plumbing, fabricated metal products*	−.0215	.0385
41 Screw machine products, etc.*	−.0191	.0423
42 Other fabricated metal products*	−.0268	.0420
43 Engines and turbines*	−.0419	.0273
44 Farm machinery, equipment*	−.0375	.0273
45 Construction machinery and equipment*	−.0047	.0391
46 Materials handling machinery and equipment*	.0000	.0491
47 Metalworking machinery equipment*	−.0034	.0564
48 Special machinery and equipment*	−.0158	.0451
49 General machinery and equipment*	−.0157	.0431
50 Machine shop products*	−.0236	.0512
51 Office, computing machines*	−.0577	.0205
52 Service industry machines*	−.0373	.0277
53 Electric transmission equipment*	−.0242	.0397
54 Household appliances*	−.0577	.0193
55 Electric lighting equipment*	−.0166	.0402
56 Radio, TV, etc. equipment*	−.0494	.0295
57 Electronic components*	−.0089	.0686
58 Miscellaneous electrical machinery*	−.0194	.0354
59 Motor vehicles, equipment*	−.0480	.0108
60 Aircraft and parts*	−.0279	.0376
61 Other transportation equipment*	−.0211	.0394
62 Professional and scientific instruments*	−.0418	.0369
63 Optical, photographic equipment*	−.0486	.0258
64 Miscellaneous manufacturing*	−.0324	.0436
65 Transportation and warehousing	−.0189	.0543
66 Communications, except broadcasting*	−.0587	.0289
67 Radio and TV broadcasting	−.0257	.0340
68 Electricity, gas, water, and sanitation	−.0670	.0111
69 Wholesale and retail trade	−.0211	.0799
70 Finance and insurance	.0000	.0804
71 Real estate and rental	−.0489	.0042
72 Hotels, repair services except auto	−.0095	.0957
73 Business services	.0000	.0634
74 Research and development	.0000	.0000
75 Auto repair services	.0000	.0264
76 Amusements	−.0169	.0500
77 Medical and educational services, nonprofit organizations	.0000	.1217
78 Federal government enterprises	−.0140	.1052
79 State and local government enterprises	−.0129	.0483

Note: Industries marked with an asterisk are those that engage in interregional trade.

This projection procedure led to some anomalous estimates for a few of the smaller industries. In the cases where the Leontief technical coefficients for labor *increased* between 1947 and 1963, a zero productivity growth rate was assumed.

Table G.1 presents the mean regional exponential rate of coefficient decline between 1947 and 1963, r, and the mean regional projected ratio of employment to output for each of the industries, $\hat{o}_{1973}$.

Appendix H

Statistical reliability of regional aggregation

The two primary data sources for this study are inconsistent in the degree of regional detail. Whereas the Current Population Survey (CPS) yields data by state, the 1960 Survey of Consumer Expenditure (SCE) was conducted in only 42 states. Moreover, problems of data reliability exist in the CPS for several of the smaller states.[1] Hence, individual states had to be aggregated into 23 regions. The 23 regions chosen are shown in Figure H.1.

Three criteria were employed in aggregating the states into regions. These were (a) consistency between data sources, (b) contiguity within a region, and (c) statistical reliability of the CPS estimate of the number of persons below the poverty line. The reason for the first criterion is obvious. The second criterion was adopted in the belief that, ceteris paribus, geographic locality affects consumption behavior—that states in close proximity to each other exhibit similar consumption behavior. The third criterion was adopted because the benefits of the policies being analyzed were aimed at the low-income population.

---

[1]Separate state data were not used because the sample was designed to provide statistically valid estimates at the regional and national levels only.

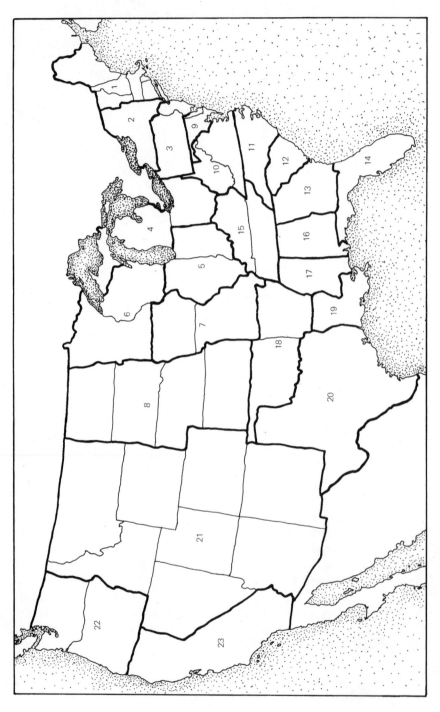

FIGURE H.1. Regions used in the analysis.

TABLE H.1
Standard errors of estimated percentages of poor persons

Estimated Percentage	Base of Estimated Percentage (in thousands)															
	200	300	400	500	750	1000	2000	3000	4000	5000	7500	10,000	20,000	30,000	40,000	50,000
1 or 99	2.13	1.74	1.51	1.35	1.10	.95	.67	.55	.48	.43	.35	.30	.21	.17	.15	.13
2 or 98	3.00	2.45	2.12	1.89	1.55	1.34	.95	.77	.67	.60	.49	.42	.30	.24	.21	.19
3 or 97	3.65	2.98	2.58	2.31	1.89	1.63	1.15	.94	.82	.73	.60	.52	.37	.30	.26	.23
4 or 96	4.19	3.42	2.97	2.65	2.17	1.88	1.33	1.08	.94	.84	.68	.59	.42	.34	.30	.27
5 or 95	4.66	3.81	3.30	2.95	2.41	2.09	1.47	1.20	1.04	.93	.76	.66	.47	.38	.33	.29
5 or 92.5	5.64	4.60	3.99	3.57	2.91	2.52	1.78	1.46	1.26	1.13	.92	.80	.56	.46	.40	.36
0 or 90	6.42	5.24	4.54	4.06	3.32	2.87	2.03	1.66	1.44	1.28	1.05	.91	.64	.52	.45	.41
0 or 80	8.56	6.99	6.05	5.41	4.42	3.83	2.71	2.21	1.91	1.71	1.40	1.21	.86	.70	.61	.54
0 or 70	9.81	8.01	6.93	6.20	5.06	4.39	3.10	2.53	2.19	1.96	1.60	1.39	.98	.80	.69	.62
0 or 60	10.50	8.56	7.41	6.63	5.41	4.69	3.32	2.71	2.34	2.10	1.71	1.48	1.05	.86	.74	.66
0	10.70	8.74	7.57	6.77	5.53	4.79	3.38	2.76	2.39	2.14	1.75	1.51	1.07	.87	.76	.68

A confidence limit of one standard deviation was accepted as a reasonable level of reliability for a region to meet criterion (c). To preserve confidentiality, the Census Bureau does not release the sampling design employed in the CPS. Hence the standard errors of the estimated percentages of poor persons could not be calculated. However, a guideline table of standard errors of estimated percentages of poor persons is provided by the Census Bureau; it is presented in Table

TABLE H.2

Estimated incidence of poverty and approximate standard errors, by region

Region	Population (in thousands)	Percentage of National Population	Estimated Incidence of Poverty	Approximate Standard Error
Northeast	49,758	23.9	9.8	.54
(1) Ct, Me, Ma, NH, RI, Vt	12,099	5.8	8.7	.58
(2) NY	18,366	8.8	10.3	.70
(3) Pa, NJ	19,293	9.3	10.0	.64
North Central	57,553	27.6	11.6	.62
(4) Oh, Mi	19,865	9.5	11.0	.64
(5) In, Il	16,542	7.9	10.4	.67
(6) Wi, Mn	8,416	4.0	10.8	.64
(7) Ia, Mo	7,636	3.7	13.4	.68
(8) Ks, Nb, ND, SD	5,094	2.4	16.4	.65
South	64,856	31.1	18.0	.66
(9) De, DC, Md	5,369	2.6	10.5	.62
(10) Va, WV	6,545	3.1	16.5	.60
(11) NC	5,214	2.5	18.9	.66
(12) SC	2,665	1.3	20.0	.64
(13) Ga	4,720	2.3	17.3	.63
(14) Fl	7,259	3.5	14.3	.63
(15) Ky, Tn	7,330	3.5	20.5	.63
(16) Al	3,510	1.7	18.8	.74
(17) Ms	2,263	1.1	34.7	.67
(18) Ar, Ok	4,612	2.2	18.5	.62
(19) La	3,720	1.8	23.5	.66
(20) Tx	11,649	5.6	16.3	.68
West	36,247	17.4	11.4	.66
(21) Az, Co, Id, Mt, NM, Nv, Ut, Wy, Ak	9,165	4.4	13.5	.66
(22) Wa, Or, Hi	6,434	3.1	14.0	.67
(23) Ca	20,648	9.8	9.8	.64
United States	208,232		13.0	

H.1. This table reveals that the standard error of an estimated percentage is less than .10 of the estimated percentage, for large population bases and large percentages. The values in italics thus satisfy the criterion. The larger the sample size and the closer the estimated percentage is to one-half, the more closely the binomial distribution approximates the normal distribution. Thus a ratio of .10 implies that if the percentage of poor persons for a region were estimated to be 10 percent, then the true percentage would lie between 9.0 percent and 11.0 percent in 68 cases out of a hundred.

Table H.2 indicates the 1973 population and the estimated incidence of poverty for the 23 regions of the study and 4 census regions, plus corresponding approximations of the standard error of the estimates. (Approximate standard errors were obtained by interpolation of Table H.1.) It may be observed that the standard error is greater than or equal to .70 for only New York and Alabama; it is greater than .66 for only 7 out of 23 regions.

Appendix I

Detailed occupational categories

The occupational categories employed in the factor employment module are aggregates of the following detailed categories used in the occupational matrix of the Bureau of Labor Statistics of the U.S. Department of Labor.

PROFESSIONAL, TECHNICAL, AND KINDRED WORKERS

Engineers, Technical
1 Engineers, aeronautical
2 Engineers, chemical
3 Engineers, civil
4 Engineers, electrical
5 Engineers, industrial
6 Engineers, mechanical
7 Engineers, metallurgical, etc.
8 Engineers, mining
9 Other engineers, technical

Natural Scientists
10 Agricultural scientists
11 Biological scientists
12 Chemists
13 Geologists and geophysicists
14 Mathematicians
15 Other natural scientists

Social Scientists
16 Economists
17 Statisticians and actuaries
18 Other social scientists

Medical and Other Health Workers

19 Dentists
20 Optometrists
21 Pharmacists
22 Physicians and surgeons
23 Veterinarians
24 Other medical and health practitioners
25 Nurses, dietitians and therapists
26 Health technicians and technicians

Teachers

27 Teachers, elementary
28 Teachers, secondary
29 Teachers, college
30 Teachers, other

Technicians, Except Medical and Dental

31 Draftsmen
32 Surveyors
33 Technicians, other engineering
34 Air traffic controllers
35 Radio operators

Other Professional, Technical, and Kindred

36 Accountants and auditors
37 Architects
38 Editors and reporters
39 Lawyers and judges
40 Librarians
41 Religious workers
42 Social and recreation workers
43 Artists and entertainers
44 Airplane pilots and navigators
45 Others

MANAGERS, OFFICIALS, AND PROPRIETORS

46 Credit men
47 Ship officers, pilots, and bursars
48 Postmasters and mail supply
49 Purchasing agents and buyers
50 Railroad conductors
51 Managers, NEC

SALES WORKERS

52 Sales workers

CLERICAL AND KINDRED WORKERS

53 Office machine operators
54 Stenographers, typists, and secretaries
55 Bookkeepers and accounting clerks
56 Bank tellers
57 Cashiers
58 Mail carriers and post clerks
59 Shipping and receiving clerks
60 Telegram and telephone operators
61 Other clerks

CRAFTSMEN, FOREMEN, AND KINDRED WORKERS

Construction Craftsmen
62 Carpenters
63 Brickmasons, stone, tile setters
64 Cement and concrete finishers
65 Electricians
66 Excavating, grading, machine operators

67 Painters, paperhangers and plasterers
68 Plumbers and pipefitters
69 Roofers and slaters
70 Others

Metalworking Craftsmen
71 Machinists and related occupations
72 Boilermakers
73 Patternmakers, metal and wood

74 Sheet metal workers
75 Toolmakers and diemakers
76 Others

Selected Printing Trades Craftsmen
77 Compositors and typesetters
78 Electrotypers and stereotypers
79 Engravers, except photoengravers

80 Pressmen and plate printers
81 Others

Selected Skilled Occupations—
Transportation, Public Utilities
82 Line and servicemen
83 Locomotive and firemen engineers

Mechanics and Repairmen
84 Airplane mechanics and repairmen
85 Motor vehicle mechanics
86 Office machine mechanics and repairmen

87 Radio and television mechanics and repairmen
88 Railroad and car mechanics and repairmen
89 Others

Other Craftsmen and Kindred Workers
90 Bakers
91 Cabinetmakers
92 Cranemen, derrickmen, hoistmen

93 Jewelers and watchmakers
94 Inspectors
95 Upholsterers
96 Others

OPERATIVES AND KINDRED WORKERS

97 Drivers, bus, truck, tractor   102 Assemblers
98 Deliverymen and routemen   103 Electroplaters
99 Brakemen and switchmen   104 Textile operatives
100 Sailors and deck hands   105 Metalworkers
101 Furnacemen and smeltermen 106 Others

LABORERS

107 Laborers, except farm

SERVICE WORKERS

108 Cleaning service workers   111 Other service workers
109 Food service workers   112 Protective service workers
110 Health service workers   113 Private household workers

FARMERS

114 Farmers and farm workers

Appendix J

Estimation of regional matrices of occupation by earnings class

As described in Chapter 4, a matrix of occupation by earnings class was applied to the vector of induced employment by occupation in order to derive a regional distribution of induced employment by earnings class. In the factor employment module, we derived a vector of induced employment demand by the 114 occupations. Call this vector L^j, for region j. Let $\mathbf{D}^j$ denote the jth region's matrix of occupation by earnings class. $\mathbf{D}^j$ is a 15×114 matrix whose typical element, d_{rs}, is the percentage of persons employed in occupation s whose earnings lie in earnings class r. In general, d_{rs} will differ by region because of regional differences in wage rates and industrial composition. If L^j is premultiplied by $\mathbf{D}^j$ and the columns of the resulting matrix are summed, a vector of regional induced employment demand by earnings class will be obtained. Call this vector $\mathbf{f}^j$. Its typical element $\mathbf{f}_r^j$ is

$$f_r^j = \sum_s d_{rs}^j \cdot l_s^j.$$

The 15 earnings classes are defined as follows, where Y is earned income (in 1969 dollars):

Earnings Class	Income
1	$Y \leq -\$2500$
2	$-\$ \ 2500 < Y \leq \$0$
3	$\$ \ 0 \quad < Y \leq \$1000$
4	$\$ \ 1000 < Y \leq \$2000$
5	$\$ \ 2000 < Y \leq \$3000$
6	$\$ \ 3000 < Y \leq \$4000$
7	$\$ \ 4000 < Y \leq \$5000$
8	$\$ \ 5000 < Y \leq \$6000$
9	$\$ \ 6000 < Y \leq \$7000$
10	$\$ \ 7000 < Y \leq \$8000$
11	$\$ \ 8000 < Y \leq \$9000$
12	$\$ \ 9000 < Y \leq \$10,000$
13	$\$10,000 < Y \leq \$15,000$
14	$\$15,000 < Y \leq \$20,000$
15	$\$20,000 < Y$

The data used to construct the $\mathbf{D}^j$ matrices were taken from the 1970 U.S. Census.[1] The data were retrieved from a magnetic tape file, available from the Census Bureau, containing a 1 percent national sample of persons and housing units drawn from the population covered by the census 15 percent sample.[2] The earners included in the tabulations were persons who claimed to have worked during the year 1969.

Tables J.1 to J.4 report the breakdown of occupation by earnings class for the four census regions—Northeast, North Central, South, and West. The eight aggregated earnings classes are as follows: $2000 or less; $2001–$3000; $3001–$4000; $4001–$5000; $5001–$6000; $6001–$10,000; $10,001–$20,000; more than $20,000. The nine occupational categories, in order, are professional, technical, and kindred workers; managers, officials, and proprietors; clerical and kindred workers; sales workers; craftsmen, foremen, and kindred workers; operatives and kindred workers; service workers; laborers, except farm and mine; and farmers and farm workers. These classes were aggregated from 114 categories employed in the analysis and presented in Appendix I.

---

[1]The sampling technique employed by the Census Bureau is reported in U.S. Bureau of the Census, *1970 Census of Population*, vol. 1, *Characteristics of the Population*, Appendix C, "Accuracy of the Data" (Washington, D.C.: U.S. Government Printing Office, 1973) (C3.223/10:970/1).

[2]More extensive information on the file may be found in the paragraph entitled "Computer Summary Tapes" in ibid., Appendix D, "Publication and Computer Summary Tape Program."

TABLE J.1

Percentage breakdown of persons employed in the Northeast, by occupation and earnings class

Occupation	Earnings Class								
	1	2	3	4	5	6	7	8	Total
1 Professional, technical, and kindred	15.29	4.73	4.73	4.48	5.06	28.52	22.02	15.29	100.0
2 Managers, officials, and proprietors	6.40	2.33	2.82	3.17	4.86	26.31	25.86	28.17	100.0
3 Sales workers	35.27	7.66	7.25	4.88	5.01	18.03	12.56	9.35	100.0
4 Clerical and kindred	26.51	8.17	9.08	12.02	13.24	25.01	4.74	1.24	100.0
5 Craftsmen, foremen, and kindred	8.90	3.14	4.11	5.03	7.83	42.14	23.63	5.23	100.0
6 Operatives and kindred	18.88	7.70	11.88	10.97	10.77	30.96	7.92	.92	100.0
7 Laborers	36.30	7.28	6.64	7.23	9.25	27.20	5.34	.77	100.0
8 Service workers	43.30	9.76	9.25	8.45	8.07	15.51	4.86	.81	100.0
9 Farmers	51.71	8.91	6.51	6.91	7.02	9.97	4.90	4.08	100.0
Total	23.33	6.64	7.59	7.87	8.71	27.02	12.49	6.35	100.0

The third census region, the South, has the largest percentage of workers with earnings less than $6000–65.7 percent as compared to 54.1 percent for the Northeast, 55.7 percent for the North Central region, and 55.0 percent for the West. This result holds consistently for workers of all occupations. For laborers, except farm and mine, the

TABLE J.2

Percentage breakdown of persons employed in the North Central region, by occupation and earnings class

Occupation	Earnings Class								
	1	2	3	4	5	6	7	8	Total
1 Professional, technical, and kindred	16.23	5.50	5.52	4.91	5.50	29.93	20.59	11.82	100.0
2 Managers, officials, and proprietors	8.34	3.06	3.53	3.90	4.83	26.56	25.72	23.96	100.0
3 Sales workers	38.51	8.09	7.27	4.92	4.49	16.13	11.93	8.67	100.0
4 Clerical and kindred	29.57	8.93	10.88	12.53	10.63	21.86	4.49	1.11	100.0
5 Craftsmen, foremen, and kindred	9.91	3.43	3.93	4.48	6.19	38.62	27.37	6.06	100.0
6 Operatives and kindred	18.92	6.70	8.08	8.40	9.07	36.16	11.27	1.42	100.0
7 Laborers	40.53	8.66	6.88	6.63	7.21	24.46	4.86	.78	100.0
8 Service workers	52.89	10.48	9.02	6.84	5.37	11.43	3.25	.72	100.0
9 Farmers	41.67	8.68	7.69	7.03	7.54	15.30	7.17	4.91	100.0
Total	26.86	7.08	7.37	7.22	7.19	26.04	12.81	5.43	100.0

TABLE J.3

Percentage breakdown of persons employed in the South, by occupation and earnings class

Occupation	Earnings Class								
	1	2	3	4	5	6	7	8	Total
1 Professional, technical, and kindred	15.46	5.31	5.69	5.66	7.80	31.33	16.60	12.14	100.0
2 Managers, officials, and proprietors	9.76	3.71	5.21	5.38	6.85	27.70	21.89	19.43	100.0
3 Sales workers	36.10	9.03	8.56	5.67	5.95	17.87	9.94	6.90	100.0
4 Clerical and kindred	29.43	9.36	13.00	14.09	10.97	18.72	3.39	1.04	100.0
5 Craftsmen, foremen, and kindred	12.83	5.41	7.65	8.89	10.88	37.25	14.49	2.59	100.0
6 Operatives and kindred	22.71	10.18	16.27	13.14	10.58	21.85	4.51	.77	100.0
7 Laborers	41.53	10.99	13.47	10.28	8.32	13.27	1.59	.56	100.0
8 Service workers	54.70	12.90	10.84	6.76	4.61	8.02	1.70	.48	100.0
9 Farmers	55.83	12.22	8.82	5.58	4.68	7.30	3.38	2.19	100.0
Total	28.66	8.74	10.58	9.25	8.48	21.64	8.28	4.36	100.0

South's percentage of workers with earnings less than $6000 is 89.8 percent as compared to 78.8 percent for the Northeast, 84.6 percent for the North Central region, and 81.8 percent for the West; for managers, officials, and proprietors, the South's share is 31.0 percent, as compared

TABLE J.4

Percentage breakdown of persons employed in the West, by occupation and earnings class

Occupation	Earning Class								
	1	2	3	4	5	6	7	8	Total
1 Professional, technical, and kindred	14.74	4.78	4.33	4.23	4.97	27.33	24.01	15.61	100.0
2 Managers, officials, and proprietors	9.98	3.05	3.76	3.76	4.84	25.13	25.20	24.08	100.0
3 Sales workers	36.48	7.58	7.31	5.51	4.92	18.07	11.57	8.56	100.0
4 Clerical and kindred	28.39	8.28	9.85	11.32	11.30	25.27	4.42	1.17	100.0
5 Craftsmen, foremen, and kindred	10.78	3.70	4.31	4.44	5.91	38.55	27.10	5.21	100.0
6 Operatives and kindred	25.14	7.68	8.62	7.84	7.67	30.38	11.12	1.55	100.0
7 Laborers	40.17	7.40	6.64	6.29	6.94	25.11	6.13	1.34	100.0
8 Service workers	49.31	10.55	9.23	7.09	5.65	12.86	4.33	.98	100.0
9 Farmers	50.87	8.93	7.80	7.57	6.12	10.78	4.34	3.59	100.0
Total	27.30	6.91	7.11	6.79	6.87	24.98	13.51	6.50	100.0

to 19.7 percent for the Northeast, 23.8 percent for the North Central region, and 25.6 percent for the West.

The North Central region has the highest percentage of earners in the category farmers and farm workers earning *more* than $6000 annually—27.4 percent as compared to 18.9 percent, 12.9 percent, and 18.7 percent for the Northeast, the South, and the West. The Northeast has the highest percentage of earners in the category managers, officials, and proprietors earning more than $6000 annually—80.3 percent as compared to 76.2 percent, 69.0 percent, and 74.4 percent for the North Central region, the South, and the West.

Appendix K

Impacts of income-transfer policies on gross output, by detailed industry

Table K.1 presents the gross output impact indicators for FAP and NIT simulations, by detailed production sectors. The sectors are those shown in Appendix G. The estimates are derived from the simulation model based on current income and marginal budget shares. The impact indicator is defined in Chapter 6, footnote 7.

TABLE K.1

Gross output impact indicators for FAP and NIT simulations based on current income and marginal budget shares, by detailed industry

Industry	FAP	NIT
1 Livestock and products	2.01	1.94
2 Other agricultural products	2.06	1.93
3 Forestry and fishery products	2.38	2.15
4 Agriculture, forestry, and fishery services	1.70	1.56
5 Iron and ferroalloy ores mining	1.37	1.30
6 Nonferrous metal ores mining	.90	.88
7 Coal mining	3.28	3.20
8 Crude petroleum, natural gas	4.29	4.05
9 Stone and clay mining	1.41	1.40
10 Chemical and fertilizer mineral mining	1.33	1.29
11 New construction	.00	.00
12 Maintenance and repair construction	1.57	1.60
13 Ordnance and accessories	−.05	−.05
14 Food and kindred products	3.14	2.90
15 Tobacco manufactures	6.45	6.20
16 Fabrics	.13	.05
17 Textile products	2.51	2.69
18 Apparel	−.78	−.83
19 Miscellaneous textile products	1.14	1.10
20 Lumber and wood products	1.29	1.31
21 Wooden containers	2.10	1.94
22 Household furniture	3.84	4.30
23 Other furniture	−.03	−.05
24 Paper and allied products	2.14	2.04
25 Paperboard containers	2.35	2.22
26 Printing and publishing	.64	.58
27 Chemicals, selected products	1.61	1.56
28 Plastics and synthetics	1.34	1.31
29 Drugs and cosmetics	4.23	4.14
30 Paints and allied products	3.77	4.02
31 Petroleum, related industry	5.26	5.03
32 Rubber, miscellaneous plastics	2.34	2.19
33 Leather tanning, products	.33	.14
34 Footwear, leather products	.36	.13
35 Glass and glass products	2.45	2.29
36 Stone and clay products	.54	.52
37 Primary iron, steel manufacturing	1.50	1.43
38 Primary nonferrous metals manufacturing	1.07	1.04
39 Metal containers	3.11	2.84
40 Heating, plumbing, fabricated metal products	.12	.12
41 Screw machine products, etc.	1.45	1.39
42 Other fabricated metal products	1.48	1.42
43 Engines and turbines	.51	.49
44 Farm machinery, equipment	−.21	−.27

TABLE K.1 continued

Industry	FAP	NIT
45 Construction machinery and equipment	.11	.10
46 Materials handling machinery and equipment	.18	.18
47 Metalworking machinery and equipment	.61	.58
48 Special machinery and equipment	.14	.13
49 General machinery and equipment	.44	.42
50 Machine shop products	1.14	1.08
51 Office, computing machines	.03	.02
52 Service industry machines	.48	.47
53 Electric transmission equipment	.47	.45
54 Household appliances	5.61	5.45
55 Electric lighting equipment	.64	.57
56 Radio, TV, etc. equipment	1.48	1.51
57 Electronic components	.93	.96
58 Miscellaneous electrical machinery	2.14	1.98
59 Motor vehicles, equipment	5.20	4.97
60 Aircraft and parts	.03	.02
61 Other transportation equipment	.36	.39
62 Professional and scientific instruments	.37	.37
63 Optical, photographic equipment	.98	1.01
64 Miscellaneous manufacturing	.63	.64
65 Transportation and warehousing	1.89	1.87
66 Communications, except broadcasting	2.03	1.88
67 Radio and TV broadcasting	.01	.01
68 Electricity, gas, water, and sanitation	1.31	1.19
69 Wholesale and retail trade	2.78	2.66
70 Finance and insurance	.29	.32
71 Real estate and rental	.38	.38
72 Hotels, repair services except auto	−.47	−.48
73 Business services	1.27	1.20
74 Research and development	.00	.00
75 Auto repair services	5.34	4.84
76 Amusements	.03	.09
77 Medical and educational services, nonprofit organizations	1.80	1.68
78 Federal government enterprises	1.36	1.30
79 State and local government enterprises	.57	.52

Appendix L

Impacts of income-transfer policies on labor demand, by detailed occupational category

Table L.1 presents the labor demand impact indicators, by detailed occupational category, for FAP and NIT Simulations I and II. The categories are those listed in Appendix I. The estimates are derived from the simulation model based on current income and marginal budget shares. The impact indicator is defined in Chapter 6, footnote 11.

TABLE L.1

Labor demand impact indicators for FAP and NIT simulations based on current income and marginal budget shares, by detailed occupational category

Occupational Category	FAP	NIT
1 Engineers, aeronautical	.50	.47
2 Engineers, chemical	1.67	1.61
3 Engineers, civil	.52	.53
4 Engineers, electrical	1.25	1.21
5 Engineers, industrial	1.35	1.31
6 Engineers, mechanical	1.18	1.14
7 Engineers, metallurgical, etc.	1.42	1.36
8 Engineers, mining	2.76	2.67
9 Other engineers, technical	1.28	1.24
10 Agricultural scientists	2.23	2.19
11 Biological scientists	1.54	1.50
12 Chemists	1.80	1.74
13 Geologists and geophysicists	2.08	2.01
14 Mathematicians	1.27	1.22
15 Other natural scientists	1.31	1.27
16 Economists	1.46	1.40
17 Statisticians and actuaries	1.18	1.15
18 Other social scientists	.73	.71
19 Dentists	1.00	.98
20 Optometrists	1.00	.98
21 Pharmacists	2.58	2.47
22 Physicians and surgeons	1.00	.98
23 Veterinarians	.98	.93
24 Other medical and health practitioners	.99	.97
25 Nurses, dietitians and therapists	1.01	1.00
26 Health technicians and technicians	.96	.95
27 Teachers, elementary	1.01	.99
28 Teachers, secondary	1.01	.99
29 Teachers, college	1.01	.99
30 Teachers, other	1.04	1.02
31 Draftsmen	1.00	.97
32 Surveyors	.48	.48
33 Technicians, other engineering	1.29	1.24
34 Air traffic controllers	.54	.54
35 Radio operators	.83	.82
36 Accountants and auditors	.98	.95
37 Architects	.13	.13
38 Editors and reporters	1.04	.95
39 Lawyers and judges	.92	.90
40 Librarians	1.01	.99
41 Religious workers	1.01	.99
42 Social and recreation workers	.43	.41
43 Artists and entertainers	.99	.96
44 Airplane pilots and navigators	1.99	1.99

TABLE L.1 continued

Occupational Category	FAP	NIT
45 Other	1.12	1.09
46 Credit men	2.05	1.97
47 Ship officers, pilots and bursars	2.30	2.32
48 Postmasters and mail supply	.53	.53
49 Purchasing agents and buyers	1.59	1.53
50 Railroad conductors	2.27	2.30
51 Managers, NEC	1.69	1.62
52 Sales workers	2.24	2.14
53 Office machine operators	1.54	1.49
54 Stenographers, typists, and secretaries	1.24	1.20
55 Bookkeepers and accounting clerks	1.65	1.59
56 Bank tellers	.56	.60
57 Cashiers	2.38	2.28
58 Mail carriers and post clerks	.53	.53
59 Shipping and receiving clerks	1.81	1.73
60 Telegram and telephone operators	1.40	1.29
61 Other clerks	1.41	1.36
62 Carpenters	.68	.69
63 Brickmasons, stone, tile setters	.59	.60
64 Cement and concrete finishers	.41	.42
65 Electricians	.99	.97
66 Excavating, grading, machine operators	.64	.64
67 Painters, paperhangers and plasterers	.64	.64
68 Plumbers and pipefitters	.79	.79
69 Roofers and slaters	.56	.57
70 Other craftsmen, foremen, etc.	1.47	1.42
71 Machinists and related occupations	1.16	1.13
72 Boilermakers	1.18	1.15
73 Patternmakers, metal and wood	1.19	1.16
74 Sheet metal workers	.98	.97
75 Toolmakers and diemakers	1.30	1.26
76 Other metalworking craftsmen	1.56	1.50
77 Compositors and typesetters	.92	.83
78 Electrotypers and stereotypers	.80	.71
79 Engravers, except photoengravers	.82	.76
80 Pressmen and plate printers	.92	.83
81 Other printing trades craftsmen	.76	.67
82 Line and servicemen	1.12	1.01
83 Locomotive and firemen engineers	2.19	2.21
84 Airplane mechanics and repairmen	1.22	1.23
85 Motor vehicle mechanics	2.63	2.50
86 Office machine mechanics and repairmen	2.53	2.41
87 Radio and television mechanics and repairmen	2.35	2.22
88 Railroad and car mechanics and repairmen	2.22	2.24
89 Other mechanics and repairmen	1.57	1.51
90 Bakers	2.82	2.68

(Continued)

TABLE L.1 continued

Occupational Category	FAP	NIT
91 Cabinetmakers	2.23	2.30
92 Cranemen, derrickmen, hoistmen	1.47	1.43
93 Jewelers and watchmakers	2.16	2.06
94 Inspectors	1.55	1.53
95 Upholsterers	2.32	2.35
96 Others	1.47	1.41
97 Drivers, bus, truck, tractor	1.89	1.86
98 Deliverymen and routemen	2.46	2.36
99 Brakemen and switchmen	2.23	2.25
100 Sailors and deck hands	2.09	2.10
101 Furnacemen and smeltermen	1.44	1.39
102 Assemblers	1.52	1.48
103 Electroplaters	1.54	1.50
104 Textile operatives	−.10	−.18
105 Metalworkers	1.85	1.78
106 Others	2.71	2.59
107 Laborers, except farm	1.42	1.39
108 Cleaning service workers	1.31	1.26
109 Food service workers	2.14	2.05
110 Health service workers	1.00	.98
111 Other service workers	.82	.78
112 Protective service workers	.58	.55
113 Private household workers	.00	.00
114 Farmers and farm workers	1.01	.95

Subject index